THE BODY OF FAITH

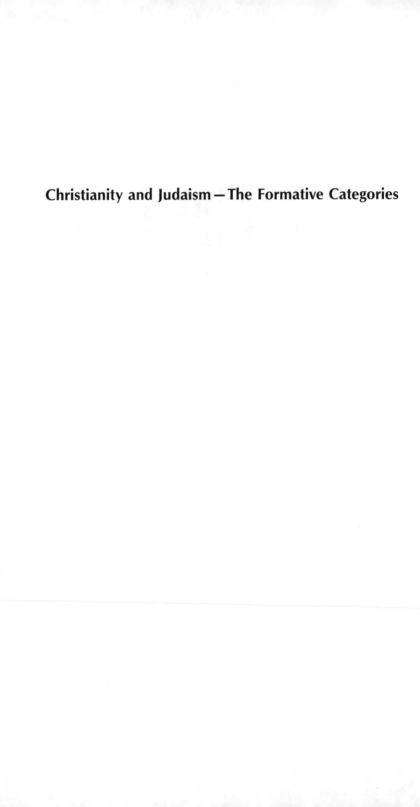

Christianity and Judaism — The Formative Categories

THE BODY OF FAITH

ISRAEL
AND THE
CHURCH

Jacob Neusner
Bruce D. Chilton

TRINITY PRESS INTERNATIONAL
Valley Forge, Pennsylvania

Trinity Press International, P.O. Box 851, Valley Forge, PA 19482-0851
Trinity Press International is part of the Morehouse Publishing Group

Library of Congress Cataloging-in-Publication Data

Neusner, Jacob, 1932–
    The body of faith : Israel and the Church / Jacob Neusner, Bruce
D. Chilton.
        p.   cm. — (Christianity and Judaism, the formative
categories)
    Includes bibliographical references and index.
    ISBN 1-56338-157-5 (pa : alk. paper)
    1. Jews in rabbinical literature.   2. Judaism—History—Talmudic
period, 10–425.   3. Rabbinical literature—History and criticism.
4. Jesus Christ—Mystical body—History of doctrines—Early church,
ca. 30–600.   5. Judaism—Relations—Christianity.   6. Christianity
and other religions—Judaism.   I. Chilton, Bruce.   II. Title.
III. Series: Neusner, Jacob, 1932–   Christianity and Judaism, the
formative categories.
BM509.J48N48   1996
296.3–dc20   96–24686

Printed in the United States of America

96   97   98   99   00   01   10   9   8   7   6   5   4   3   2   1

Contents

Preface

Christianity and Judaism, along with Islam, by their own word seek to reach the same God, but each takes its own path. All three invoke the same authority, Abraham and Sarah, represented by the same Scripture, and all three worship the one and only God, concurring that the God of which the one speaks is the same God that the others adore. At the same time, each distinguishes itself from the other two, finding important differences at specific points and maintaining that it, and not the others, accurately records what the one, unique God has said. Sustained argument takes place when people who agree on premises and principles also disagree on propositions and conclusions, and therefore Judaism, Islam, and Christianity can sustain — and for determinate periods in the past did mount — cogent and illuminating arguments against one another.

Among the three, because of the intimacy of their relationship — historical and geographical alike — Judaism and Christianity have formed the closest relationships, which, in the very recent past, have turned cordial. In the past, the relationship was one of contempt and incomprehension, each for the absurdities of the other. Imputations of guilt, recriminations, not to mention exclusion and even murder, ruined the possibilities of mutual illumination of self-respecting and mutually honored partners in dialogue. Now, for the first time in the United States and in the English-speaking world in general, differences between those two complex sets of religious traditions come under discussion free of rancor and recrimination. Consequently, outlining the points of concurrence and conflict may take place in a spirit of enlightenment and friendship, not to negotiate, or even place limits upon, difference, but only to understand the other more fully and more accurately.

Our purpose here is to compare and contrast the paramount theological categories of Judaism and Christianity, each meaning to inform the other of the main points of the classical theology of his religious tradition on matters of concern to the other. Each, moreover, takes seriously and comments upon the other's presentation, observing similarity and difference. So we mean to describe, then compare and contrast, the main theological structures on which our respective faiths are constructed.

We do not propose to obscure theological difference or to sidestep profound disagreement in quest of the socially useful goal of amity. To the contrary, we seek a different goal from theological negotiation; neither is "liberal" about his own beliefs, let alone "tolerant" of the choices made by the other. Each believes in his tradition and its affirmations, and each without apology or excuse practices that tradition. Neither proposes to permit long-term friendship and partnership in intellectual projects to impose conditions on the integrity of his faith, nor wants the other to. Both of us are educators and scholars, firm in the conviction that knowledge and understanding affirm our convictions but also yield respect for differing ones. We each seek to grasp the rationality of the views of the other, in full awareness that it is a different rationality.

The present work is one of the three volumes that together constitute the series we have entitled Christianity and Judaism — The Formative Categories. In the series, we propose to provide the faithful of both Judaism and Christianity with an informative, factual account of how, in their classical formulations, Christianity and Judaism addressed the same issues and set forth their own distinctive programs and sets of propositions. This is plausible and productive for several reasons.

First, Jews and Christians have lived side by side for nearly two thousand years; each group knows a great deal about the other. We have been neighbors for a long time, and now we are striving to become friends. While neither proposes to surrender the slightest point of distinctiveness, while both affirm the ultimate difference of the one from the other, and while both parties differ about how we know the same God and about what that God has made manifest to us — we concur that we really do worship the same God. Hence, the possibility of educating ourselves about the other emerges: we disagree about the same things while also agreeing in many areas.

Second, because Christianity and Judaism in structure and even system are so much alike, it is possible to compare their theological formulations of the same questions. Because they so vigorously disagree on the main points, it is productive and interesting to do this, though we do not mean here to carry forward the centuries-old disputations between the two great religious traditions of the West.

Third, because Christianity and Judaism (along with Islam) today confront as partners the challenges of militant secularism and proselytizing atheism, we find ourselves drawn together to address a common enemy. From the late eighteenth century to nearly our own day, practitioners of Judaism stood by while ethnic Jews allied the Jewish population with militant secularism. Nearly all Jews, including practitioners of Judaism ("Judaists"), took for granted, and with ample cause, that only in a neutral, secular society could Jews survive as a distinct group and that only in a neutral political world could Judaism be practiced. Moreover, communal secularism within Jewry held together the religious sector of the community, the Judaists, and the secular sector, the solely ethnic Jews. Only in the most recent past has a different perspective on the imperatives of the public square reshaped this vision; now a growing minority within the Jewish community finds friends outside not among militant secularists but in Christians of goodwill — Roman Catholic, Protestant, and Orthodox. With them Judaists make common cause in a number of shared projects, even while carefully agreeing to set aside all theological discourse. The Judaic partner in these books concurs with this minority view. Judaists and Christians, loyal to their respective faiths, recognize urgent, shared commitments to the social order.

Now this very new, but very promising, recognition of mutuality of interest calls for precisely the kinds of books that we — the two authors of these volumes — mean to write together. For mutuality of interest depends in the end upon mutuality of understanding. By that we mean that we simply have to get to know one another better than we now do. The shared labors for the public interest are best carried out by people who, agreeing to disagree on some things and to work together on others, deeply respect and fully understand the difference that separates them. And that requires knowledge, not the pretense that some subjects lie beyond all discourse. Precisely what the body of Christ means to the Christian, or the election of Israel (the holy people) to the Judaist, what the Torah tells the Judaist and the Bible the Christian, how God is made manifest in this world, that is, is "incarnate," to both Judaist and Christian — these fundamental points of commonality in structure, conflict, and system require exposition, and we promise that exposition in these books.

Ours is not a relationship of sentimentality or careful avoidance of difference. We do not believe that, at the foundations, we really are the same thing, and neither wants to become like the other or to give up any part of what makes him different from the other in the most profound layers of conviction and calling. The one writer is called to the study of the Torah as his way of life and purpose of being; the other is called to understand how God may be embodied within human living. But for the one, the study of the Torah, and for the other, the divine incarnation that Jesus Christ makes possible, carry learning beyond the boundaries of the Torah or of Christ, respectively. Each finds his work possible only through learning more about the religion of the other. And both maintain that sound learning and authentic understanding of their respective faiths demand attention to the near-at-hand religion of the other.

Still, we work together in a personal, not a theological, partnership. The two authors are longtime friends, and we come together in an irenic spirit, genuinely fond of each other and also respectful of the call that each acknowledges God has vouchsafed to the other. We cannot explain how God has spoken in such different terms to so many people. We do not know why God has made us so different from each other — all the while seeking to serve that one and the same true God. But we know that within the traditions that shape our lives and minds, we are constrained to recognize that the other is possessed of the same revelation that we revere. Since the Judaic partner understands that Christianity's "Old Testament" is his "written Torah," and since the Christian partner recognizes the same fact, both share the common ground that here God has said the same thing to each, and on that account comparison and contrast form options that we now wish to explore.

Firm in our convictions, neither of us asks the other to surrender his beliefs; we are not going to say which of us, from God's viewpoint, is right. In the fullness of time God will not only decide but make the decision known. For the interim we accept the situation of indeterminacy: each of us is sure he is right, but neither finds the other's assent — therefore, conversion — a condition of mutual education. There is a very practical reason for that shared decision, even while for the two of us it also represents a dimension of religious conviction to leave for God the final choice.

If we do not choose here to debate who is right, it is in some part because that debate has gone on through long centuries, and we doubt much is left to be said. Nor has the debate proved illuminating or productive, when framed in terms of truth and error. But we do wish to provide for faithful believers in Judaism and Christianity a systematic and fair-minded picture of what both religions say about the same things. The differences coincide: Torah or Bible (volume 1), Israel or Church (volume 2), the media of God's this-worldly incarnation (volume 3). In our view, religious dialogue, including debate, benefits us all. Our theory — and here we speak only for ourselves personally, and not for the Church or the Torah — is that each has learned something about God that the other must want to know, even while each of us knows full well that the criterion of truth rests, as it has always rested, for Judaism with the Torah, and for Christianity with the Christ. But that candid affirmation of difference defines not the end but only the beginning of the dialogue that we believe finally serves the greater glory of the one God who has been made manifest to us all not only in different ways but, through Scripture, in one and the same way too.

For both value "the Book," meaning, the Hebrew Scriptures of ancient Israel. What that means should be made clear, since the issues that divide us are theological and not exegetical. Many hold that because Judaism and Christianity share the

same Scriptures — the written Torah and the Old Testament being mostly concentric — the debate between them concerns the
meaning of those writings. We take a different view. Our commonalities and differences do not involve only how we read the
received and revealed Scriptures but what we know about God.
Although such knowledge is, to be sure, related to those Scriptures, it derives from theology, not from literary criticism or the
exegesis of sources.

That is why we frame our comparisons in theological terms:
revelation of God, the body of faith, the presence of God in
the world, rather than in the contrasts between one party's
reading of pertinent verses of Scripture and the other party's
reading of those same verses. The reason is that theology does
not recapitulate Scripture, but the exegesis of Scripture recapit-
ulates theology. The further reason is that for neither party is
the Scripture of ancient Israel the sole and complete account
of God's revelation to humanity. Christianity requires the New
Testament, Judaism, the oral part of the Torah; so the issue is
not exegetical at all. The issue is how we fill with meaning
the shared and common generative categories of the theological
structure on which both build their systems: God, Torah, Israel
for Judaism; God, Christ, Church for Christianity.

We underline, therefore, that for each of us, Israelite Scripture, though held in common, is contingent, because each of us
complements the shared Scriptures with further revelation. Judaism knows those Scriptures as the written part, which, along
with the oral part, comprises the one whole Torah that God gave
("revealed") to Moses, our rabbi, at Mount Sinai. Christianity knows those same Scriptures as the Old Testament, which,
along with the New Testament, comprises the Bible, the word
of God. Because of the rich heritage of Scripture, with its ethics
and morality and its account of what God wants of humanity,
who God is, and what we are, many have concluded that a unitary "Judeo-Christian tradition" defines the common religion of
the West; Judaism and Christianity then are supposed to differ
on details but concur on the main points. The opposite is the
fact, and here we propose a different reading of the relationship
between the two heirs of ancient Israel in the West.

Specifically, we spell out how, because they concur on so

much, the two religious traditions differ in a very explicit and precise way. They talk about the same things; they invoke the same evidence; they rest their respective cases on the same premises of thought and rules of argument. And they profoundly differ. They divide on precisely what unites them, and their shared agenda of faith in and love for God accounts for the vigor and precision of their disagreements. That is to say, Judaism and Christianity identify the same principal and generative categories for the formulation of the religious life: revelation, social order, and the encounter with God. In Judaism, these categories bear the titles "Torah," "Israel," and "God in this world," which, in the classical documents of formative Judaism, encompasses diverse ways in which we meet God in the here and now. In Christianity, the counterparts are "the Bible," "the Church," and "Christ Incarnate."

In these three volumes, therefore, we identify and spell out in an elementary way the three principal areas of communion among, and therefore conflict between, the heirs of the same Scripture:

1. how and what we know about God, that is, the character of revelation;

2. who constitutes the people to whom God is made manifest, that is, the definition of the body of the faithful; and

3. where and through whom we meet God in this world.

Each religious tradition sets forth its definition of revelation; each defines the social order to which God has spoken, called into being in God's service; and each knows where and how, in this world, we meet God in human encounter.

We focus on the classical and definitive documents of the two traditions. For Judaism, this involves the following: the Torah, as it took shape in the first six centuries of the Common Era, as the source of revelation; the same writings' account of who and what is "Israel"; and those documents' exposition of ways in which, in everyday life, God enters into the situation of ordinary people: how we meet God this morning, right here. For Christianity, the counterpart categories address the distinct issue of how and where God is revealed in his fullness, as the divine King who is to be all in all. The New Testament represents a dynamic development, within a period of about seventy years, from a local movement that operated within an agreed understanding of Israel to an international movement that begged the question of just what "Israel" might mean. Unless that development is appreciated, one cannot understand Christianity. Both authors elect to limit discussion to the classical writings, in the clear recognition that both religions unfolded through time, so that later writers expanded and recast the classical definitions and even categories. But we maintain that, however things changed through time, the classical formulation remains paramount.

We mean to speak to Jews and Christians who want better to understand their own religious traditions. In our view, when we identify the issues that theological teachings address and understand the alternative positions on those issues that classical thinkers have adopted for themselves, we treat religion as vital. We cease to regard our views as self-evident and recognize that the religious decisions made by Jews and Christians represent choices made in full consideration of alternatives. Then our respective religions take on weight and consequence and become living choices among alternative truths. Only by seeing the options that have faced the framers of Judaism and Christianity in their classical writings shall we understood how, in full rationality and with entire awareness of issues and options, the founders of our respective traditions took the paths they did. When religion is reduced to platitudes and banalities, lifelessly repeating things deemed to be self-evident, it loses all consequence and forms a mere chapter in the conventions of culture. But from Judaism and Christianity, for centuries stretching backward beyond counting, faithful Israel, on the one side, and the living body of Christ, on the other, drew sustenance and found the strength to endure.

Let us not at the end lose sight of the remarkable power of these religions in times past and in our own day. The world did not make life easy for Judaism through its history in the West; and in the age of militant secularism, on the one side, and violently anti-Christian Communism, on the other, Christianity has found itself back in the catacombs. The century that now closes has afforded to the faith of Israel and of Christ no honor, and to the Israelite and to the Christian no respect by reason of loyalty to that vocation. Christianity outlived Communism in the Soviet Union and its colonies. At the sacrifice of home and property, even at the price of life itself, Israel resisted the world's corrosive insistence that it cease to exist and has reaffirmed its eternal calling. Whatever the choice of private persons, that social order formed by Israel, on the one side, and the Church of Jesus Christ, on the other, has endured against it all, despite it all, through all time and change. Defying fate in the certainty of faith in God's ultimate act of grace is the one thing God cannot have commanded, but it is what, in times of terrible stress, Judaic and Christian faithful have given freely and of their own volition. God can have said, and did say, "Serve me," but God could only beseech, "And trust me too."

For even God cannot coerce trust. Only Israel and the Church could give what God could ask but not compel: the gifts of the heart, love and trust, for which the loving God yearns, which only the much-loved Israel or those who have been called into the Church's community can yield freely, of their own volition. And that is what Israel, in response to Sinai, and Christendom, in response to the empty tomb, willingly gave, and by their loyal persistence freely give today. These facts of human devotion tell us the power of the faiths that in these pages meet for a theological comparison. The stakes then are very high indeed.

The joint authors express their thanks to their respective academies, Bard College and the University of South Florida, for ongoing support for their scholarly work. At these academies, each has found ideal conditions for a life of learning, and neither takes for granted the gifts that he receives in these centers of higher learning. Both express thanks, also, to Dr. Harold Rast, publisher of Trinity Press International, for his commitment to this project and his guidance in bringing it to fruition. If we achieve our goal of a sustained and illuminating theological encounter, it is because of his guidance and long-term commitment to our project.

•

Lastly, we would like to call attention to our complementary project, *Judaeo-Christian Debates: Communion with God, the Kingdom of God, the Mystery of the Messiah,* scheduled for publication by Fortress Press in 1997. The two projects are readily distinguished. In the present one, we compare and contrast the principal components of the counterpart structures of Judaism and Christianity, and in the other we do the same for the counterpart systems of the two traditions. Here, in these three volumes, we spell out how the two faiths compare when set forth side by side; in the companion work, we explain how they function in comparable, sometimes parallel, ways: how each brings about communion with God, how each defines the worldly life of the faithful under God's dominion, and how each addresses the issue of teleology through the medium of eschatology. We express our thanks to the publishers of both projects for their willingness to let us do the work in the way that we have devised.

BRUCE CHILTON
Bard College

JACOB NEUSNER
*University of South Florida
and Bard College*

Introduction

Religion and Community in Judaism and Christianity

While religions speak to individuals in the privacy of their hearts, they also define themselves through social entities. Whether these take the form of Church, holy people, nation of Islam, or kingdom of God, they are always defined by appeal to religious conviction. So the theory of the social entity of a religious system, which we may call an *ethnos*, leads us into the religious structure as surely as the doctrine of God or the explanation of how we know about God in revelation.

This brings us to "Israel" in Judaism and Christianity. The reason that the definition of Israel bears considerable weight in the theology of Judaism is simple. The Torah revealed by God to Moses at Sinai is given to Israel, the holy people. When Jews call themselves Israel, their initial claim is that they constitute that Israel to whom God gave the Torah. So the identification of Israel in the theology of Judaism, as much as in the politics of the Jews in the contemporary world, forms a weighty and crucial consideration, a fundamental component of the theology of Judaism. And, as a matter of fact, all those who inherit the Hebrew Scriptures of ancient Israel that Judaism calls "the written Torah," specifically, the Christians, who revere the written Torah as "the Old Testament," also claim to form (an) Israel, because they receive these Scriptures. The earliest Christians insisted that they were part of Israel, or the true Israel, and for many centuries, as we shall see later on, that point of insistence formed a principal issue between Judaism and Christianity. It

1

must follow that when we speak of Israel, we address not only the facts of sociology but the truths of theology.

We should not confuse theological theories of the body of believers with the facts of sociology. The *ethnos* of a religious system defines the social entity that embodies the religious system's way of life and worldview. The theory then governs how a social entity — people who see themselves as belonging together — views itself. For example, a systemic social entity comes into being when villagers see themselves as "Israel" or as "the body of Christ." The fundamental social unit in Israelite society in the Land of Israel in ancient times was the household, encompassing the large-scale economic unit of the farmer, his wife and children, slaves, and dependent craftsmen and artisans, reaching then outward to other such households to form a neatly composed social unit, the village, and reaching finally outward to other similar villages. Judaism's systemic social entity transformed the extended family into a representation, in the here and now, of mythic Israel. That is, Jews here and now continue that Israel of which the ancient Scriptures speak. In that way, the social unit adopted for itself and adapted for its purposes the social entity of Scripture and identified itself with the whole life and destiny of that entity. Clearly, therefore, Judaism set forth a theory of the ethnic entity that invoked a metaphor in order to explain the group and identify it. That fundamental act of metaphorization, from which all else follows, was the comparison of persons (Jews) of the here and now to the Israel of which the Hebrew Scriptures (the Torah) speak, and the identification of those Jews with that Israel. Treating the social group — two or more persons — as other than they actually are in the present, as more than a mere given, means that the group is something else than what it appears to be.

Christianity's systemic social entity emerges not from an overt desire to define Israel as such but from the need to express how God can be understood to make himself known to diverse peoples. Jesus' public ministry offered the benefits of the kingdom to those at the margins of Judaism and even to some considered foreign to Judaism. The success of the preaching about Jesus among non-Jews then raised the question of the continuity between Jesus' kingdom and Israel in an acute form. The issue of how such diversity can be incorporated into what is still a single *corpus* — Israel — has been and remains central within Christianity. To explain what is at stake in the categories *ethnos*/"Israel" and *ethnos*/"Church," we have to recognize that the raw materials of the definition are not the facts of the social order but the imaginations of the system-builders. Here we will formulate matters in terms of Israel, but it is easy enough to translate this formulation into Christian terms. A theory of Israel — that is, a theory of what Israel is and who is counted as part of it — in any Judaic system finds its shape and structure within that system. That Israel takes shape out of materials selected by the systemic framers from a miscellaneous and received or invented repertoire of possibilities. It goes without saying that, in the context of the description of the structure of a Judaism, its "Israel" is the sole Israel (whether social group, caste, family, class, "population," or any of the many other social entities admirably identified by sociology) defined by that Judaism. The best systemic indicator is a system's definition of its Israel, and Judaisms, or Judaic systems, from the priests' pentateuchal system onward made their statement principally through their response to the question framed in contemporary Judaic and Jewish-ethnic discourse as "Who is a Jew?"

If it is true that the definition of the systemic component, *ethnos*, is shaped within the systemic imagination, not out of the raw materials of the social world beyond the system, then a system never accommodates the givens of politics and of an external and encompassing society. The notion that society gives birth to religion is systemically beside the point. Systems do not recapitulate a given social order; rather, they define one, and their framers, if they can, then go about realizing their fantasy. An Israel within a given Judaic system presents traits that the system-builders deem self-evidently true, without regard to realities beyond the range of systemic control. All that the context presents is a repertoire of possibilities. The framers of the contents then make their choices among those possibilities, and, outside of the framework of the system, there is no predicting the shape and structure of those choices. The system unfolds within its own inner logic, making things up as it goes along — because it knows precisely how to do so.

The Judaism of the dual Torah put forth two major theories regarding who and what Israel is: one in the Mishnah, a philosophical law code (ca. 200 C.E.), the other in the Talmud of the Land of Israel (Yerushalmi) and related writings (ca. 400 C.E.). When the Mishnah was written, Christianity had not yet attained legal status, but when the Talmud of the Land of Israel was produced, Christianity not only was licit but was becoming the official religion of the Roman Empire. What was ignored in 200 formed a formidable challenge two hundred years later. The first Judaic theory of Israel took shape outside of the relationship to the advent of Christianity, the second theory explicitly responded to Christians' claims that they also constituted "Israel."

Israel as Holy People

The Mishnah took shape at a time at which Christianity formed a minor irritant, perhaps in some places a competing Judaism, but not a formative component of the social order, and certainly not the political power that it was to become. Hence the Mishnah's framers' thinking about Israel in no way took account of Christianity's competing claim to form the true Israel; Israel remained intransitive, bearing no relationships to any other distinct social entity. The opposite of "Israel" in the Mishnah is "the nations," on the one side, or "Levite, priest," on the other: always taxonomical, never defined out of relationship to others within the same theoretical structure. As we shall see, the opposite of "Israel" in the Yerushalmi became "Rome," and Israel found itself defined as a family, with good and bad seed. Now the nations were differentiated, and a different world-order conceived; Israel entered into relationships of comparison and contrast, not merely hierarchy, because Christianity, sharing the same Scriptures, now called into question the very status of the Jews to constitute Israel.

The Mishnah defines "Israel" as bearing two identical meanings: the Israel of all the Jews here and now, but also the Israel of which Scripture — the Torah — spoke. And these meanings encompass both the individual and the group, without linguistic differentiation of any kind. Thus in the Mishnah, "Israel" may refer to an individual Jew (always male) or to "all Jews," that is, the collectivity of Jews. The individual woman is nearly always called *bat yisrael* (daughter of [an] Israel[ite]). Sages in the Mishnah did not merely assemble facts and define the social entity by simply describing the given. Rather, they portrayed it as they wished to. They imputed to the social group, Jews, the status of a systemic entity, Israel. To others within Jewry it was not at all self-evident that "all Jews" constituted one Israel and that that one Israel formed the direct and immediate continuation, in the here and now, of the Israel of holy writ and revelation. As we shall see, the Essene community at Qumran did not come to that conclusion, and the sense and meaning of "Israel" proposed by the authorship[1] of the Mishnah and related writings did not strike Philo as the main point. Paul, for his part, reflected on Israel within categories not at all symmetrical with those of the Mishnah.

The mishnaic identification of Jewry in the here and now with the Israel of Scripture therefore constituted an act of metaphor, comparison, contrast, identification, and analogy. It is a daring social metaphor. Implicitly, moreover, the metaphor excluded a broader range of candidates from the status of (an) Israel, the Samaritans being one example, the scheduled castes of Mishnah tractate Qiddushin (chap. 4) being another. Calling (some) Jews "Israel" established the comprehensive and generative metaphor that gives the mishnaic system its energy. From that metaphor all else derived momentum.

The Mishnah defines "Israel" in antonymic relationships of two sorts: first, Israel as against not-Israel, Gentile; and, second, Israel as against priest, or Levite. Israel serves as a taxonomic indicator, specifically part of a more encompassing system of hierarchization. On the one hand, Israel defined the frontiers on the outer side of society; on the other hand, it defined the social boundaries within society. To understand the meaning

---

1. The character of the Mishnah mirrors its purpose: it presents itself as the work not of individual authors but of a collective, anonymous "authorship."

of "Israel" as the Mishnah and its associated documents of
the second and third centuries sort matters out, we must consider the sense of "Gentile." The authorship of the Mishnah
does not differentiate among Gentiles, who represent an undifferentiated mass. To the system of the Mishnah, whether
or not a Gentile is a Roman or an Aramaean or a Syrian or
a Briton does not matter. That is to say, differentiation among
Gentiles rarely, if ever, makes a difference in systemic decision
making.

But it is also true that to the system of the Mishnah, Israel,
as regards the relationship at hand, is not differentiated either.
The upshot is that just as "Gentile" is an abstract category, so is
"Israel." *Kohen* (priest) is a category, and so is "Israel." For the
purposes for which Israel/priest are defined, no further differentiation is undertaken. That is where for the mishnaic system
matters end. But to the Judaic system represented by the Yerushalmi and its associated writings, "Gentile" may refer to Rome
or other-than-Rome, for instance, Babylonia, Media, or Greece.
That act of further differentiation — we may call it "specia-
tion" — makes a considerable difference in the appreciation of
the Gentile. In the Mishnah's authorship's Israel, therefore, we
confront an abstraction in a system of philosophy.

If we measure the definition against the social facts in the
world beyond, we see a curious contrast. The Mishnah's systemic categories within "Israel" did not encompass the social
facts that required explanation. Two hundred years later, however, two metaphors, rarely present and scarcely explored in the
Mishnah and associated documents, came to prominence in the
Talmud of the Land of Israel. These were, first, the view of Israel as a family, the children and heirs of the man Israel; and,
second, the conception of Israel as sui generis. While "Israel" in
the first phase of the formation of Judaism perpetually found
definition in relationship to its opposite, "Israel" in the second phase constituted an autonomous entity, defined in its own
terms and not solely or mainly in relationship to other comparable entities. The enormous investment in the conception of
Israel as sui generis makes that point blatantly and provides the
confidence to use comparison in order to assert the ultimate autonomy of Israel. But Israel as family bears that same trait of

autonomy and self-evident definition. Curiously, confidence in Israel as sui generis resulted in the transitive contrast between Israel and other groups.

Israel as a Family

The genealogical Israel in the second stratum of the canon of the Judaism of the dual Torah bears a socially vivid sense. Now Israel forms a family, and an encompassing theory of society, built upon that conception of Israel, permits us to describe the proportions and balances of the social entity at hand, showing how each component both is an Israel and contributes to the larger composite as well. Israel as sui generis carried in its wake a substantial doctrine of definition, a weighty collection of general laws of social history governing the particular traits and events of the social group. In comparing intransitive to transitive Israel, we move from Israel as not-Gentile and Israel as not-priest to powerful statements of what Israel is. It is necessary, then, to specify in concrete terms the reasons adduced to explain the rather striking shift before us. Two important changes account for the metaphorical revolution at hand, one out at the borders of, the other within, the Jews' group.

By claiming that Israel constituted "Israel after the flesh" — the actual, living, present family of Abraham and Sarah, Isaac and Rebecca, Jacob and Leah and Rachel — Talmudic sages met head-on the Christian claim that there was (or could ever be) some other Israel, of a lineage not defined by the family connection at all, and that the existing Jews no longer constituted Israel. By representing Israel as sui generis, sages moreover focused upon the systemic teleology, with its definition of salvation, in response to the Christian claim that salvation is not of Israel but of the Church, now enthroned in this world as in heaven. The sage — the model for Israel, a model based on Moses, our rabbi — represented on earth the Torah that had come from heaven. Like Christ, on earth as in heaven, like the Church, the body of Christ, ruler of earth (through the emperor) as of heaven, the sage embodied what Israel was and was to be. So Israel as family in the model of the sage, like Moses, our rabbi, corresponded in its social definition to the Church of Jesus Christ, the New Israel, the source of salvation of humanity. The metaphors given prominence in the late fourth- and fifth-century sages' writings formed a remarkable counterpoint to the social metaphors important in the mind of significant Christian theologians, as both parties reflected on the political revolution that had taken place.

In response to the challenge of Christianity, the sages' thought about Israel centered on the issues of history and salvation, issues made not merely chronic but acute by Christianity's political triumph. That accounts for the unprecedented reading of the outsider as differentiated, a reading contained in the two propositions concerning Rome: first, Rome, as Esau or Edom or Ishmael, seems to be part of the family; second, Rome is "the pig." Differentiating Rome from other gentile places represented a striking concession indeed, without counterpart in the Mishnah. Rome is represented as only Christian Rome can have been represented: it looks kosher, but it is unkosher. Pagan Rome cannot ever have looked kosher, but Christian Rome, with its appeal to ancient Israel, could and did and moreover claimed to. However, while it bore some traits that validate this claim, it lacked others.

The metaphor of the family proved equally pointed. Sages framed their political ideas within the metaphor of genealogy because, to begin with, they appealed to the fleshly connection, the family, as the rationale for Israel's social existence. A family beginning with Abraham, Isaac, and Jacob, Israel could best sort out its relationships by drawing into the family other social entities with which it found it had to relate. So Rome became the brother. That affinity came to light only when Rome had turned Christian, for Christian Rome shared with Israel the common patrimony of Scripture — and said so. The character of the sages' thought on Israel therefore proved remarkably congruent to the conditions of public discourse that confronted them.

The Issue of Israel in Other Systems Set Forth by Heirs of Ancient Israel

The Israel of Judaism answers the larger question that other components of that same Judaism — its theory of revelation, its account of how we know God in the world — address. And that is so in other systems as well: the definition of "Israel" forms an integral part of a larger statement, and that statement's theological logic dictates the character of its Israel. We see this is so when we turn to Paul's Israel, the Israel of the Greek-speaking Jewish philosopher Philo of Alexandria, the Israel of the Essene community of Qumran, and other systems. The comparison provides perspective on the entire issue of how Christianity and Judaism defined the community of the faithful, the body of believers.

Paul's Israel

The shape and meaning imputed to the social component, Israel, conform to the larger interests of the system and in detail express the system's main point. We see this when we contrast the Israel of Rabbinic Judaism with the Israel of Paul's thought. In his representation of his Israel, Paul presents us with a metaphor for which, in this context, there is no counterpart in the documents of the Judaism of the dual Torah. Israel compared to an olive tree, standing for Israel encompassing Gentiles who believe but also Jews by birth who do not believe; Israel standing for the elect and those saved by faith and therefore by grace — these complex and somewhat disjoined metaphors and definitions form a coherent and simple picture when we see them not in detail but as part of the larger whole of Paul's entire system. For the issue of Israel for Paul forms a detail of a system centered upon a case in favor of salvation through Christ and faith in him alone, even without keeping the rules of the Torah.

The generative problematic that tells Paul what he wishes to know about Israel derives from the larger concerns of the Christian system he proposes to work out. That problematic was framed in the need, in general, to explain the difference, as to salvific condition, between those who believed and those who did not believe in Christ. Specifically, it focused upon how those who believed in Christ but did not derive from Israel related to both those who believed and also derived from Israel and those who did not believe but derived from Israel. Do the first-named have to keep the Torah? Are the nonbelieving Jews subject to justification? We may take for granted that Paul's own Jewish origin made the question at hand important, if not critical. What transformed the matter from a chronic into an acute question — the matter of salvation through keeping the Torah — encompassed, also, the matter of who is Israel.

For his part, Paul appeals, for his taxic indicator of "Israel," to a consideration we have not found commonplace at all, namely, circumcision. The necessity of circumcision is certainly implicit in the Torah, but the Mishnah's laws accommodate as Israel persons who (for good and sufficient reasons) are not circumcised and treat as "not-Israel" persons who are circumcised but otherwise do not qualify. So for the Mishnah's system, circumcision forms a premise, not a presence, a datum, not a decisive taxic indicator. Paul, by contrast, called all those who are circumcised Israel and all those who are not circumcised "not-Israel" — pure and simple. Jonathan Z. Smith states:

> The strongest and most persistent use of circumcision as a taxic indicator is found in Paul and the deutero-Pauline literature. Paul's self-description is framed in terms of the two most fundamental halakhic definitions of the Jewish male: circumcision and birth from a Jewish mother.... "Circumcised" is consistently used in the Pauline literature as a technical term for the Jew, "uncircumcised," for the Gentile.[2]

It must follow that for Paul, Israel is "the circumcised nation," and "an Israel" is a circumcised male.

Smith spells out the reason for the meaning attached to Israel: "What is at issue . . . is the attempt to establish a new taxon:

---

2. Jonathan Z. Smith, "Fences and Neighbors," in *Approaches to Ancient Judaism,* ed. W. S. Green (Missoula, Mont.: Scholars Press, 1978), 2:12; also in Jonathan Z. Smith, *Imagining Religion: From Babylon to Jonestown* (Chicago: University of Chicago Press, 1982), 1–18.

'where there cannot be Greek and Jew, circumcised and un-circumcised, barbarian and Scythian' (Col. 3:11), 'for neither circumcision counts for anything, nor uncircumcision, but a new creation' (Gal. 6:15)."[3] It follows that for Paul, the matter of Israel and its definition forms part of a larger project of reclassifying Christians in terms not defined by the received categories: Paul (as we recall from chap. 1 of Romans) is speaking of a third race, a new race, a new man, in a new story. Smith proceeds to argue that the matter is entirely explicit in Paul's larger system:

> Paul's theological arguments with respect to circumcision have their own internal logic and situation: that in the case of Abraham, it was posterior to faith (Rom. 4:9–12); that spiritual things are superior to physical things (Col. 3:11–14); that the Christian is the "true circumcision" as opposed to the Jew (Phil. 3:3).... But these appear secondary to the fundamental taxonomic premise, the Christian is a member of a new taxon.[4]

In this same context, Paul's letter to the Romans presents a consistent picture. In chapters 9 through 11, Paul presents his reflections on what and who is (an) Israel. Having specified that the family of Abraham will inherit the world not through the law but through the righteousness of faith (Rom. 4:13), Paul confronts Israel as family and redefines the matter in a way coherent with his larger program. He states that the children of Abraham will be those who "believe in him that raised from the dead Jesus our Lord, who was put to death for our trespasses and raised for our justification" (Rom. 4:24–25). The critical issue here is whether or not Paul sees these children of Abraham as Israel. The answer is in his address to "my kinsmen by race." There, in Romans 9, he writes that those kinsmen are Israelites, "and to them belong the sonship, the glory, the covenants, the giving of the law, the worship, and the promises; to them belong the patriarchs, and of their race, according to the flesh, is the Christ. God who is over all be blessed for ever" (Rom. 9:3–4). Israel then is the holy people, the people of God.

---

3. Ibid., 12 (in *Approaches to Ancient Judaism*).
4. Ibid.

But Paul proceeds to invoke a fresh metaphor (commonplace in the rabbinic writings later on, to be sure), of Israel as olive tree, and so to reframe the doctrine of Israel in a radical way: "Not all who are descended from Israel belong to Israel, and not all are children of Abraham because they are his descendants; ... it is not the children of the flesh who are the children of God, but the children of the promise are reckoned as descendants" (Rom. 9:6–7). Here we have an explicit definition of Israel, now not after the flesh but after the promise. Israel then is no longer a family in the concrete sense in which, in earlier materials, we have seen the notion. "Israel after the flesh" who pursued righteousness that is based on law did not succeed in fulfilling that law because they did not pursue it through faith (Rom. 9:31), "and Gentiles who did not pursue righteousness have attained it, that is, righteousness through faith" (Rom. 9:30). Now there is an Israel after the flesh but also "a remnant, chosen by grace; ... the elect obtained it [righteousness]" (Rom. 11:5–7). The consequence of this is that the fleshly Israel remains, but Gentiles ("a wild olive shoot") have been grafted "to share the richness of the olive tree" (Rom. 11:17). Do these constitute Israel? Yes and no. They share in the promise. They are Israel in the earlier definition of the children of Abraham. There remains an Israel after the flesh, which has its place as well. And that place remains with God: "As regards election they are beloved for the sake of their forefathers. For the gifts and the call of God are irrevocable" (Rom. 11:28–29).

The shape and meaning imputed to the social component Israel here conform to the larger interests of the system constructed by Paul, both episodically and, in Romans, quite systematically. Israel as a detail also expresses the system's main point. For Paul's Judaic system, encompassing believing (former) "Gentiles" but also retaining a systemic status for non-believing Jews, Israel forms an important component within a larger structure. More to the point, "Israel" finds definition on account of the logical requirements of that encompassing framework. Indeed, there is no making sense of the remarkably complex metaphor introduced by Paul — the metaphor of the olive tree — without understanding the problem of thought that confronted him and that he solved through, among other details, his thinking on Israel. The notion of entering Israel through belief but not behavior ("works") in one detail expresses the main point of Paul's system, which concerns not who is Israel but what faith in Christ means.

Israel in the Thought of Philo

For Philo, Israel forms a paradigmatic metaphor, bearing three meanings. The first is ontological and signifies the place of Israel in God's creation. The second is epistemological. This signifies the knowledge of God that Israel possesses. The third is political, referring to the polity that Israel possesses and projects in light of its ontological place and epistemological access to God. Our point of interest begins to come into focus when we perceive even from a distance the basic contours of Philo's vision of Israel. What we shall see is that, for Philo, Israel formed a category within a larger theory of how humanity knows divinity, an aspect of ontology and epistemology. What makes an "Israel" into Israel for Philo is a set of essentially philosophical considerations, concerning adherence to or perception of God. In the philosophical system of Philo, Israel constitutes a philosophical category, not a social entity in an everyday sense.

That is not to suggest that Philo does not see Jews as a living social entity, a community. The opposite is the case. His *Embassy to Gaius* is perfectly clear that the Jews form a political group. But that fact makes no difference to Philo's philosophical Israel. For when he constructs his philosophical statement, the importance of Israel derives from its singular capacity to gain knowledge of God that other categories of the system cannot have. When writing about the Jews in a political context, Philo does not appeal to their singular knowledge of God, and when writing about the Jews as Israel in the philosophical context, he does not appeal to their forming a this-worldly community. That again illustrates the claim that it is within the discipline of its own logic that the system invents its Israel, without responding in any important way to social facts out there, in the larger world.

Seeing Israel as "the people which is dedicated to his [God's] service," Philo holds that Israel is the best of races and is capable of seeing God, and this capability of seeing God is based upon Israel's habit of service to God.[5] The upshot of this is the capacity to receive a type of prophecy that comes directly from God; thus one must be descended from Israel to receive that type of prophecy. An Egyptian, Hagar, cannot see the Supreme Cause. The notion of inherited "merit" (in this context an inappropriate metaphor) bears more than a single burden; here merit or inherited capacity involves a clearer perception of God than is attained by those without the same inheritance — a far cry indeed from the "merit of the ancestors" as the fourth-century sages would interpret it. Mere moral and intellectual qualifications, however, do not suffice. One has to enjoy divine grace, which Moses had and which, on account of the merit of the patriarchs, the people have.

The Israel of the Essene Community of Qumran

When the framers of the documents of the Essene library of Qumran use the term "Israel," they are referring to the members of the community itself — and no one else. They start with that "us" and proceed from there to "Israel." In this way, as with the documents of the second phase of the dual Torah, the movement of thought began with the particular and moved outward to the general. The group's principal documents were the Community Rule, which "legislates for a kind of monastic society"; the Damascus Rule, which outlines "an ordinary lay existence"; and the War Rule and Messianic Rule, which, "while associated with the other two, and no doubt reflecting to some extent a contemporary state of affairs, plan for a future age."[6] Among the four, the first two offer us their framers' understanding of the relationship between "us" (that is, the people of the community) and "Israel."

Stated simply, what these documents meant by "us" was simply "Israel" or "the true Israel." The group did not recognize

5. H. A. Wolfson, *Philo* (Cambridge, Mass.: Harvard University Press, 1962), 51–52.
6. Geza Vermes, *The Dead Sea Scrolls: Qumran in Perspective* (Philadelphia: Augsburg, 1981), 87.

other Jews as Israel. That is why the group organized itself as a replication of "all Israel," as they read about Israel in those passages of Scripture that impressed them. They structured their group, in Geza Vermes's language, "so that it corresponded faithfully to that of Israel itself, dividing it into priests and laity, the priests being described as the 'sons of Zadok' — Zadok was High Priest in David's time — and the laity grouped after the biblical model into twelve tribes." This particular Israel then divided itself into units of thousands, hundreds, fifties, and tens. The Community Rule describes divisions within the larger group, specifically, "the men of holiness" and "the men of perfect holiness." The corporate being of the community came to realization in common meals, prayers, and deliberations. Vermes says, "Perfectly obedient to each and every one of the laws of Moses and to all that was commanded by the prophets, they were to love one another and to share with one another their knowledge, powers, and possessions."[7] The description of the inner life of the group presents us with a division of a larger society. But — among many probative ones — one detail tells us that this group implicitly conceived of itself as Israel.

The group lived apart from the Temple of Jerusalem and had their liturgical life worked out in utter isolation from that central cult. They had their own calendar, which differed from the one observed in general, for their calendar was reckoned not by the moon but by the sun. This yielded different dates for the holy days and effectively marked the group as utterly out of touch with other Jews.[8] Because the Essene community at Qumran followed a solar calendar, their holy days were working days for others and vice versa. The group furthermore had its own designation for various parts of the year. The year was divided into seven fifty-day periods, each marked by an agricultural festival, for example, the Feast of New Wine, The Feast of Oil, and so on. On Pentecost, treated as the Feast of the Renewal of the Covenant, the group would assemble in hierarchical order: "the priests first, ranked in order of status, after them the Levites, and lastly 'all the people one after another in their Thousands,

---

7. Ibid., 89.
8. Ibid., 176.

Hundreds, Fifties, and Tens, that every Israelite may know his place in the community of God according to the everlasting design."[9] There can be no doubt from this passage — and a vast array of counterparts can be assembled — that the documents at hand address Israel.

The Israel of the Essenes is the Israel of history and of the eschatology of Scripture, as much as the Israel of the authorship of the Yerushalmi, Genesis Rabbah, and Leviticus Rabbah refers back to the Israel of Genesis and Leviticus. The other Israel — Philo's — comprises people of shared intellectual traits in a larger picture of how God is known, as much as the Israel of the authorship of the Mishnah and related writings exhibits taxonomic traits and serves a function of classification. Both sets of politicians present us with political "Israels," that is, each with an Israel that exhibits the traits of a polis, a community (a people, a nation). Both sets of philosophers offer a philosophical Israel, with traits of a taxonomic character — one set for one system, another set for the other — that carry out a larger systemic purpose of explanation and philosophical classification.

The Body of Faith and the Place of Israel in a Judaic Religious Structure

Now we ask: Just how important is Israel to the several Judaic religious systems, inclusive of Paul's, that define their *ethnos,* or theory of the social entity, in these terms? The criterion of importance does not derive from merely counting up references to Israel. Rather, to assess the role and place of the social entity in a system, we must ask a simple question: Were the entity or trait "Israel" to be removed from a given system, would that system radically change in character, or would it merely lose a detail? What is required is a mental experiment, but not a very difficult one. What we do is simply present a reprise of our systemic description. When that is done, three facts emerge.

First, without an "Israel," Paul would have had no system. The generative question of his system required him to focus

---

9. Ibid., 178.

attention on the definition of the social entity Israel. Paul's system originated among Jews but addressed both Jews and Gentiles, seeking to form the lot into a single social entity "in Christ Jesus." The social dimension of his system formed the generative question with which he proposed to contend.

Second, without an "Israel," Philo, by contrast, could have done very well indeed. For even our brief and schematic survey of Philo has shown us that Israel did not matter to his overall scheme. It was a detail of a theory of knowledge of God, not the generative problematic even of the treatment of the knowledge of God, let alone of the system as a whole (which we scarcely approached and had no reason to approach!). We may therefore say that Israel formed a systematically important category for Paul but not for Philo. Accordingly, the judgment of the matter rests on more than mere word-counts, on the one side, or exercises of impression and taste, on the other. It forms part of a larger interpretation of the system as a whole and what constitutes the system's generative problematic.

Third, if we were to remove "Israel" in general and in detail from the topical program of the Essenes of Qumran, we should lose, if not the entirety of the library, then nearly the whole of some documents, and the larger part of many of them. The Essene library of Qumran constitutes a vast collection of writings about Israel, its definition and conduct, history and destiny. We cannot make an equivalent statement about the entire corpus of Philo's writings, even though Philo obviously concerned himself with the life and welfare of the Israel of which, in Alexandria as well as elsewhere, he saw himself a part. The systemic importance of Israel for the Essenes of Qumran derives from the meanings imputed to that category. The library stands for a social group that conceives of itself as Israel and that wishes, in these documents, to spell out what that Israel is and must do. The system as a whole forms an exercise in the definition of "Israel" as against that "non-Israel" composed not of Gentiles but of erring former Israelites. The saving remnant — Israel — is all that is left.

Paul's context told him that Israel constituted a categorical imperative, and it also told him what he had to discover about Israel in his thought on the encounter with Christ. The Essenes of Qumran by choice isolated themselves and in that context made a determination about the generative issue of describing an Israel that, all by itself in the wilderness, would survive and form the saving remnant.

Paul — all scholarship concurs — faced a social entity ("Church" or "Christian community") made up of Jews but also Gentiles, and some of those Jews expected people to obey the law, for example, to circumcise their sons. Given the natural course of biological life, that was not a question to be long postponed, which imparts to it the acute, not merely chronic, character that it clearly displayed even in the earliest decade beyond Paul's vision. And that fact explains why, for Paul, circumcision formed a critical taxic indicator in a way in which, for Philo, for the Mishnah, and for other Judaic systems, it did not.

The circumstance of the Essenes of Qumran is far better documented, since that community through its rereading of Scripture tells us that it originated in a break between its founder(s) and other officials. Consequently, characterizing the Essenes of Qumran hardly moves beyond the evidence in hand. They responded to their own social circumstance, isolated and alone as it was, and formed a community unto itself, hence seeing their Israel, the social entity of their system, as what was left of Scripture's Israel, that is, the remnant of Israel.

The sages of the Judaism of the dual Torah, whose Judaic systems are set forth in the Mishnah, Midrash, and Talmuds, made their documentary statements in reply to two critical questions, the one concerning sanctification, presented by the final failure of efforts to regain Jerusalem and restore the Temple cult, the other concerning salvation, precipitated by the now-unavoidable fact of Christianity's political triumph.

The State of Israel Today

This discussion of the various conceptions of Israel throughout history leads us now to the confusing fact that "Israel" in Judaism refers to the holy people of God, children of Abraham, Isaac, and Jacob, who stood with Moses at Sinai and received the Torah and entered the covenant with God, while "Israel" in the world today refers to the State of Israel. People today think of Israel as the Jewish state in the Land of Israel (aka, Palestine), a political entity, equivalent to the United States. But in Judaism, "Israel" has a different meaning altogether, a transcendent, supernatural significance: "people of God," "holy people," "children of Abraham, Isaac, and Jacob," and equivalent theological formulations.

We have therefore to realize that, when we study Judaism, we are dealing not with the Jews as a diverse set of ethnic groups but with "Israel" as a theological formation, corresponding in the here and now to those Jews who identify themselves as practitioners of Judaism. It is somewhat complicated to realize that a religious community, "Israel," and an ethnic group or set of ethnic groups, "the Jews," coincide. That is because while all Judaists, or practitioners of Judaism, also are by definition Jews, members of the ethnic group, not all Jews are Judaists. If we define a Jew as the child of a Jewish mother (that is the definition of the law of Judaism) who either practices Judaism or does not practice any religion, then matters become clearer. All such Jews of ethnic definition may without an act of conversion adopt Judaism as their religion; all other human beings may adopt Judaism as their religion only through an act of conversion.

In the theology of Judaism, "Israel" has carried a variety of meanings, and each of these served not as a concrete description of real people living in the here and now, a merely factual statement of how things are, but as a metaphor. The metaphor took on genealogical, political, supernatural, taxonomical, hierarchical, ontological, or epistemological character, as systems varied. Not only so, but this Israel enjoyed no counterpart among social entities here on earth; as sui generis, Israel framed its own (of necessity, unintelligible) metaphor. This social entity, this Israel, therefore may constitute a family of a particular order — that is, all Jews descend from Abraham, Isaac, and Jacob, Sarah, Rebecca, Leah, and Rachel. Thus we invoke the metaphor of family.

Or, it may be held, Israel constitutes a people or a nation, in which case to be Israel is to be part of a political unit of one kind or another, comparable to other such social groups based on, or in, a shared political being, and that will dictate thought about the nature of Israel, about whether or not the Jews at a given time and place constituted a political entity at all. We also find, in contrast, the claim that the social entity at hand simply is not like any other, is a genus unto itself. Israel as "unique" has no counterpart among the nations; on one side of the social equation of humanity are all the nations all together, on the other side, Israel, all alone. These and other metaphors serve as the vehicles for the social thought of the Judaic systems, or Judaisms, of the ages. These abstract observations have now to be made concrete for a Judaism.

While in today's world it is taken for granted that the word "Israel" refers to "the Jewish people," we Jews define our most vexed issues in terms of the questions Who is Israel? (that is, Who is a Jew?) and What is Israel? (that is, Where should Jews live? What kind of a social entity do they, and should they, constitute?). Not only so, but when the founders of the Jewish state called it "the State of Israel," they made a powerful statement indeed. What they said was that "to be 'Israel' " means to form a political entity, a state, the Jewish state, the Jewish state located in the Land of Israel. Then those who do not live in that place fall outside of Israel (that is, "the State of Israel"). Clearly, therefore, when in contemporary Jewish discourse people talk about Israel, they mean a variety of things and deliver a considerable judgment indeed.

Just as in today's world the word "Israel" commonly is made to refer to the State of Israel, so the word "Israeli" is commonly used to designate a citizen of that nation. "Israel" also may refer to a particular place, namely, the territory of the State of Israel, the Land of Israel. But that narrow and particularly political, enlandised, and empowered meaning is new, beginning, as it does, in 1948. Long prior to that time, and even today, there has been a second and distinct meaning: "Israel" as "all Jews everywhere," the people of Israel. This definition of "Israel" as "the Jewish people" (sometimes spelled with a capital *P*: "the Jewish People") identifies Israel with a transnational community. It is a very important meaning of the word, for Scripture's many references to Israel, as in "the Guardian of Israel does not slumber or sleep," then are taken to refer to that people (or People).

Throughout the liturgy of the synagogue, "Israel" always refers to the people, wherever they live, and not to the State of Israel today.

The fact that these two meanings, the one particular to a state, the other general to a scattered group, contradict each other alerts us to a problem. It is that a single word may stand for two things. And, as we shall see in the pages of this book, it may stand for many more. Indeed, thinking about Israel leads us deep into the generative processes of the theology of Judaism. In their reflection on that to which Israel is to be compared and contrasted; in their selection, from a repertoire of metaphors available from Scripture, of a particular set of comparisons; in their mode of thought on the matter, whether philosophical and abstract, whether political and concrete, our sages of blessed memory tell us the fundamental affirmation of the theology of Judaism: land, state, people — Israel all.

Part One

Israel:
God's Stake
in History

JACOB NEUSNER

1

Israel in the Theology
of Judaism

The definition of "Israel" is a central element in the theology of
Judaism, and the same holds true for Christianity's definition of
"Church." These definitions explain who the members are when
they join together into a group they hold to be select, different
from all others, and holy. When people explain to themselves
the character and calling of the social entity that they comprise
and the life they lead together, they may compose for themselves an encompassing picture. We call this picture a "system"
when it is composed of three necessary components: an account
of a worldview, a prescription of a corresponding way of life,
and an understanding of the social entity that is defined by the
first component and described by the second. When those three
fundamental components fit together, they sustain one another
in explaining the whole of a social order, hence constituting the
theoretical account of a system. Systems defined in this way
work out a cogent picture, for those who make them up. That
picture comprises *how* things are correctly to be sorted out and
fitted together, explains *why* things are done in one way rather
than in some other, and defines *who* they are that do and understand things in this particular way. When, as is common, people
invoke God as the foundation for their worldview, maintaining
that their way of life corresponds to what God wants of them,
projecting their social entity in a particular relationship to God,
then we have a religious system.

When people call themselves "Israel" and mean by that the
same group of which the Hebrew Scriptures (or "Old Testa-

ment") speak, they claim for themselves a standing and a status
that the simple facts of daily life do not, and cannot, validate.
This is an act of theological faith, not sociological description.
They compare themselves to some other social group and allege
that they are like that other group or continue it or embody it
in the here and now. In explaining who they are, they evoke
what we may call a social metaphor. For the statement "We are
Israel" means to allege "We are like the Israel of old," the Israel
of which the Scriptures speak. The same is so when Christians
of a given locale call themselves "the Church" or "the body
of Christ." They speak of what is not seen, though it is very
real. In both of these cases, the claims — that "we" are Israel
or that "we" are the body of Christ — involve metaphors invoked to explain the character and standing of a social entity.
Social metaphors therefore involve the things to which a group
of people compare themselves in accounting for their society
together.

"Israel" — that is, a theory of who "we" are in relationship
to the Israel of the Torah — is the basic and required element
of all theology of Judaism. There can be no Judaism without a
clear statement of who and what is Israel. The identification of
Israel has preoccupied thinkers of all Judaisms from the beginning to the present. The making of Judaic systems commenced
with the formation of the Pentateuch in the aftermath of the destruction of the First Temple of Jerusalem in 586 B.C.E. From that
time to the present, the definition of "Israel" — who belongs,
who does not, and what sort of social entity Israelites adhere to
in forming (an) "Israel" — has formed a remarkably pervasive
theme in all Judaisms. The systemic treatment by a Judaism of
the category "Israel" is one critical and indicative issue of a Judaic system under study. The centrality of thought on Israel for
all Judaisms from their beginnings to now may be assessed in
part by examining the record of the past, but there is more to
it than that.

For the theology of Judaism, the definition of an "Israel"
takes the form of spelling out the rules of relationship. To define one social entity, an "Israel," the sages of the Judaism of
the dual Torah not only explain how that entity relates to some
other but also compare and contrast that entity to some other.

Accordingly, when the sages wish to think about Israel or "an Israel," their ordinary mode of thought is to ask to what Israel or an Israel is to be compared, hence in what ways it is like, and in what ways it is unlike, that to which it is compared. These then form the contrastive and analogical processes of reflection — metaphorical thinking.

How come Israel, the social group imagined as a principal component of the formation of all of creation, took such a prominent place in the theology of Judaism? The reason is that the doctrine of what is Israel and who is Israel, as worked out over seven hundred years, held the whole system together. The story begins with the reconstitution of the Jews in the Land of Israel some three generations after the destruction of the First Temple in 586 B.C.E. The urgency of the issue Israel may be explained by reference to the reconstruction of the story of the group accomplished, out of materials referring to the period before 586, by authorships after that turning point.

Specifically, that point of entry into reflection on the issues of group life — the identification of an appropriate definition, a social metaphor for the group — was dictated by the interpretation placed upon the events of the sixth century by the emergent Scripture, the Pentateuch (or Five Books of Moses). That document, composed in part from revised materials deriving from the period before the destruction in 586, treated as critical the issues of the ongoing life of the community, seen as not a given but a gift, and its relationship to the land that it possessed, interpreted as subject to diverse stipulations. The upshot was the doctrine of the experience of exile and return, and that doctrine imparted to the social entity formed by the Jews of the Land a heightened reality, treating as problematic and uncertain what, in the view of others, was simply another fact of the social life of humanity in that region.

In other words, because many of the formative events — the destruction of the First Temple in 586 B.C.E., the return to Zion in 450 B.C.E., the rebuilding of the Temple, and the promulgation of the Torah of Moses as the governing document — involved tumult and disorientation, the theme of identity became critical. The authorship of Scripture took this unsettling and disorienting experience and composed an account of Israelite society.

It selected as normative two experiences: the exile from Jerusalem and destruction of the Temple; and the return to Zion and rebuilding of the Temple. The paradigm of exile and return made it difficult to think of the life of the group as a given, a fixed star in the firmament of reality. Rather, that unsettling account of the life of the group portrayed the group's collective existence as a gift and not a given, as something subject to stipulations and conditions, for example, a covenant with God. The terms of the covenant — involving the moral traits of life on the land, the uncertainty of the ongoing existence of the group unless certain conditions were met, and the notion that the group came from somewhere and was en route to some further destination — highlighted the issue of who is Israel and what an Israel is.

That framing of events into this pattern represents an act of powerful imagination and interpretation, a symbolic transaction. Diverse experiences have been sorted out; various persons have been chosen; and the whole has been worked into a system by those who selected history out of happenings and models out of masses of persons. I say "selected" because no Jews after 586 B.C.E. actually had experienced what in the aggregate Scripture says happened. None both went into exile and then came back to Jerusalem. So, to begin with, Scripture does not record a particular person's experience. It is not autobiographical. Further, it also is not an account of a whole nation's story; the original exile encompassed mainly the political classes of Jerusalem and some useful populations alongside. Many Jews in the Judaea of 586 never left. And, as is well known, a great many of those who ended up in Babylonia stayed there. Only a minority went back to Jerusalem. Consequently, the story of exile and return to Zion encompasses what happened to only a few families, who identified themselves as the family of Abraham, Isaac, and Jacob; their genealogy became the history of Israel. Had the Torah been written by the families that stayed and by those that never came back, it would have told a normative and paradigmatic tale that was altogether different.

That experience of the few that formed the paradigm for Israel beyond the restoration taught lessons of alienation as normative. Let me state with emphasis the lessons people claimed to learn out of the events they had chosen for their history: the life of the group is uncertain, subject to conditions and stipulations; *nothing* is set and given; *all things* are a gift: land and life itself. But what actually did happen in that uncertain world — exile but then *restoration* — marked the group as special, different, select.

There were other ways of seeing things, and the pentateuchal picture was no more compelling than any other. Those Jews who did not go into exile and those who did not "come home" had no reason to take the view of matters that characterized the authorship of Scripture. The life of the group need not have appeared more uncertain, more subject to contingency and stipulation, than the life of any other group. The land did not require the vision that imparted to it the enchantment, the personality, that, in Scripture, it received: "The land will vomit you out as it did those who were here before you." And the adventitious circumstance of Persian imperial policy — a political happenstance — did not have to be recast into return. So nothing in the system of Scripture (exile for reason, return as redemption) followed necessarily and logically. Everything was invented: interpreted, much as with the force and power of metaphor.

The paradigm was shaped from the experience of the uncertainty of the group in the century or so from the destruction of the First Temple of Jerusalem by the Babylonians in 586 to the building of the Second Temple of Jerusalem by the Jews who returned from exile with Persian permission and sponsorship. Following the promulgation of the Torah of Moses under the sponsorship of Ezra, the Persians' viceroy, around 450 B.C.E., all future Israels would refer to that formative experience as it had been set down and preserved in the mythic terms of that "original" Israel — the Israel not of Genesis and Sinai, ending at the moment of entry into the promised land, but the Israel of the families that recorded the story of both the exile and the return as rule and norm. That minority genealogy — that story of exile and return, alienation and remission, imposed on the received stories of preexilic Israel, adumbrated time and again in the Five Books of Moses, and addressed by the framers of that document in their work over all — is the paradigmatic statement in which every Judaism, from then to now, has found its structure and deep syntax of social existence, the grammar of its intelligible message.

To be (an) "Israel" — the social component of a Judaism — from then to now has meant to ask what it means to be Israel. The original pattern meant that an Israel would be a social group whose existence had been called into question and affirmed — and therefore always would be called into question and would remain perpetually to be affirmed. Every Judaism then would have the task of recapitulating the original Judaism. That is to say, each would make its own distinctive statement of the generative and critical resentment contained within that questioning of the given, that deep understanding of the uncertain character of the existence of the group in its normal location and under circumstances of seeming permanence, circumstances that (so far as the Judaic group understood things) characterized the life of every other group but Israel. What for everyone else (so it seemed to the Judaisms addressed to the Israels through time) was a given, for Israel was a gift. What all the nations knew as how things *must* be, Israel understood as how things *might not be*. While the nations knew permanence, Israel knew exile and loss, alienation and resentment. But it also — in the stead of annihilation — knew renewal, restoration, reconciliation, and (in theological language) redemption. So that paradigmatic experience, the one beginning in 586 and ending around 450, written down in that Torah of Moses, made its mark. That pattern, permanently inscribed in the Torah of God to Moses at Sinai, would define for all Israels over all time the matter of resentment demanding recapitulation: leaving home, coming home. An Israel — any Israel — would then constitute a social entity engaged by exile and return. But that covered a wide range of possibilities. The most important possibilities were fully realized in the theology of Judaism: Israel as holy people, Israel as extended family, Israel as sui generis, Israel as different from the rest of all humanity, non-Israel.

2

Israel as Kingdom of Priests and Holy Nation

The doctrine of Israel implicit throughout the Mishnah, which was compiled around 200 C.E., and explicit in many of its details may be stated very simply: the community now stands in the place of the Temple of Jerusalem, destroyed in 70 C.E. What that meant is that the social entity Israel would now serve as the Temple had. The Temple walls had marked the boundaries between holy and ordinary. So now did Israel. As in the vision of Ezekiel in chapters 40–47, the Temple had marked the boundaries among the levels of society, with the high priest going to the innermost sanctum, then the priests going closest to the holiest place, with others at distances determined by rank: first Levites, then Israelite males, then women, and on outward. So now did the social entity Israel serve this inner-facing task of social hierarchization, as well as the outer-facing task of political differentiation of "Israel" from everyone else, "the nations."

"Israel" was both a genus and a species: it was a species of the genus "people" or "nation," and it was a genus possessing only one species — itself. The true nature of Israel was thus murky, convoluted, complex, and the issue of who and what is Israel profoundly troubled the Mishnah's authorship. The question provoked sustained thought, which is revealed in the points of emphasis of the Mishnah's theology as a whole. The holiness of the life of Israel, the people, a holiness that had formerly centered on the Temple, now endured and transcended the physical destruction of the building and the cessation of sac-

31

rifices. The Mishnah's theology stated in countless details that Israel the people was holy, was the medium and the instrument of God's sanctification.

What required sanctification, in particular, were the modalities of life lived in community: procreation, nourishment, family, land, time, village, temple. The system instructed Israel to act as if "Israel" (the Jewish people), like the Temple of old, formed a utensil of the sacred. Two points of ordinary life formed the focus for concrete, social differentiation in the foundations of the Mishnah's theology of sanctification: food and sex, the latter governing valid marriage. What people ate, how they conducted their sexual lives, and whom they married or to whom they gave their children in marriage would define the social parameters of their group. These facts indicate who was kept within the bounds and who was excluded and systematically maintained at a distance. That is why and how sanctification functions to define the social thinking and therefore to lend shape to metaphors of the social entity of a system.

How does this work in detail? The word and category "Israel" reach definition in relationship to other species of its genus: if Israel is viewed as a "nation," then it is defined as being "not-Gentile"; if it is viewed in terms of caste, then it is defined as being "not-priest." These definitions, based in this-worldly terms, self-evidently tell us much about what Israel is when compared with other nations or other castes, but nothing about what Israel *is*. That is what we mean by Israel as intransitive and not transitive. In the theology of the Mishnah, "Israel" draws upon metaphors of a hierarchical character — nation, caste — while "Israel" in the pages of the Talmud of the Land of Israel and related Midrash compilations appeals to concrete, societal, or familial metaphors, or is represented as utterly other and (by means of explicit comparisons) sui generis.

In the Mishnah, the term "Israel" also serves in such phrases as "Land of Israel," "house of Israel," "son of Israel," "daughter of Israel," and so on. Other examples are the following: the laws of Israel, offspring of Israel, elders of Israel, seed of Israel, wisdom of Israel, congregation of Israel, strength of Israel, myriads of Israel, first born of Israel, virgin of Israel, redeemer of

Israel, border of Israel, great ones of Israel, fields belonging to Israelites, mountains of Israel, camp of Israel, community of Israel, dead of Israel, tribes of Israel, youths of Israel, vengeance of Israel, princes of Israel, sight of Israel, sustainers of Israel, army of Israel, needs of Israel, shepherds of Israel, remnant of Israel, tribes of Israel, guardian of Israel, and on and on. All of these usages are the same as in "king of Israel." They bear the simple sense of "belonging to the social entity, Israel"; that is, "daughter of Israel" means simply a Jewish woman, though it can bear the sense "a woman of the Israelite, not the priestly caste." The adjectival usage is neutral, not categorical. In all of these adjectival usages, "Israel" has an implicit meaning that derives from the contexts in which the word is given one or the other meanings deriving from relationship. My impression is that nearly all adjectival uses of " . . . of Israel" bear the sense of the particular people Israel: that is, they refer to that group of people who are not not-Israel.

While in Scripture, and later on in the Talmud Yerushalmi and related writings, Israel is treated as an extended family, the Mishnah's authorship rarely makes use of that category. Like Israel sui generis, the meaning of "Israel" as family when it does occur always bears supernatural, not narrowly familial or genealogical, meaning or occurs in a liturgical context, which is the same thing. When terms like "fathers" or "ancestors" are joined to the noun "Israel," a supernatural sense intrudes: for example, "God of the fathers of Israel" (M. Bik. 1:4); or "All Israelites are sons of princes" (which is ordinarily understood to allude to their being children of Abraham) (M. Shab. 14:4) — this for purposes of ritual classification. Not every genealogical reference demands the sense of "family": for example, "the children of Israel" (M. Neg. 2:1) is simply synonymous with "Israel" the social entity, pure and simple. These usages are not commonplace and play no role in the formulation of the law, to which the bulk of the Mishnah is devoted.

When the framers of the Mishnah use the word "Israel," they may well mean "the people of God," "your people," and the like. In that usage, "Israel" refers to a supernatural social entity, one that stands in a special relationship with God and addresses God on distinctive terms. Like the reference to Israel as sui generis, such nongeneric usages most commonly occur in liturgical settings: for example, "Save, O Lord, your people, the remnant of Israel" (M. Ber. 4:4); and "Let us bless the Lord, our God, the God of Israel" (M. Ber. 7:3). In relationship to God, Israel always bears a supernatural dimension: for example, "So too, the Holy One, blessed be he, purifies Israel" (M. Yoma 8:9); "The Holy One, blessed be he, found as a utensil to hold a blessing for Israel only peace" (M. Uqs. 3:12). But we do not know any other term the people could have used to refer to themselves as a group in a secular sense. They would, then, have used this same word that bore a supernatural component: "Israel." In short, the word "Israel" in liturgy does not function in a way different from the way it serves in a sentence on how one Israelite's cow gored another "Israel's" cow.

That is why these merely episodic occurrences of the term "Israel" in a supernatural sense do not bear deep significance in the metaphorical treatment of an abstract entity. Rightly understood, the supernatural dimensions and considerations pertinent to this Israel indeed encompass the bulk of the rules of the Mishnah, even where "Israel" does not occur in so many words. And where "Israel" serves as antonym for "Gentile," the sense, even when neutral, bears subterranean meaning of a supernatural order. For example, the statement "An Israelite may not raise pigs in any location" (M. San. 7:7), a rule that bears the sense, "but a Gentile may do so," carries no explicit explanation, but the implicit sense, that the Gentile is not subject to those rules of heaven that make Israel what it is, everywhere prevails. Along these same lines, "An Israelite may lend at usury the capital of a Gentile with the Gentile's knowledge and consent" (M. B.M. 5:6) stands for a more than merely ethnic difference.

The single most common antonym for "Israel" is "not-Israel," that is, Gentile. But — and this is important — that usage need not evoke invidious comparisons, which is why the ubiquitous premise of Israel as unique and holy makes so slight a contribution to our understanding of the Mishnah's definition and utilization of the social metaphor at hand. Far more commonly than otherwise, "Israel" is the name of the social group, pure and simple. For example, "Israel" may refer to the people without bearing any supernatural sense: for example, "So that the poor people of Israel may rely upon it in the Seventh Year..." (M. Yad. 4:3); "...so that the last of Israel may reach the Euphrates" (M. Ta. 1:3); "He who sees a place in which miracles were done for Israel..." (M. Ber. 9:1). When one wishes to speak of the distinct social entity, the Jews, the word "Israel" serves in a perfectly routine and neutral way; it does not mean "Israel-by-contrast-to-Gentiles" any more than it means "Israel-by-contrast-to-priests." For example, M. Sot. 1:8 refers to "the heart of Israel," meaning the people at large. "The stoning of the felon is done by all Israel" (M. San. 6:4) refers simply to "everybody present." "For from there Torah goes forth to all Israel" (M. San. 11:2) again refers to "the entirety of the nation."

If one wishes to impute the sense "every individual Israelite," the essentially secular and ordinary meaning does not shift. "Israel" may refer to the people, without bearing a supererogatory sense. "When Israel came up from the exile" (M. Sheq. 2:4) refers to "the Israelites" in general. So too, "So as not to frighten Israel..." (M. Yoma 5:1); "Happy are you, O Israel..." (M. Yoma 8:9); "Even though Israel requires his services..." (M. Mak. 2:7); "Even the general of the army of Israel such as Joab..." (M. Mak. 2:7) — all refer to Israelites as a social entity. In public worship, "Israel" may refer equally to the community at large or to the caste, the Israelites, in particular. As to the former, an example is: "The Israelites answered Moses, 'Amen'" (M. Sot. 5:4). A further example is at M. R.H. 3:8: "Until the Israelites went up from Jerusalem to the Temple Mount," which refers to "everybody," the entire group, the community at large; so too, "The court goes and all Israel after them..." (M. Sheb. 2:2). That particular usage bears no sense of exclusion; that is, it does not mean "the Israelites alone, and not the Gentiles, the Samaritans, the priests...," though in other contexts it assuredly does have such a meaning. As mentioned above, Israelite women are invariably called "daughters of Israel" (e.g., M. Ned. 9:10; M. Yeb. 13:1), meaning simply "Jewish women," and that usage too bears no exclusionary sense, except, now, for Gentiles. When "Israel" is used as a geographical indicator, the sense is "a place populated by Israelites." "In all the towns of Israel" (M. Zeb. 14:7) refers to all towns in which Israelites make up the inhabitants or the majority thereof.

While "Israel" therefore is the name of the social entity to which the Mishnah's authorship addresses its system, the fact remains that for the authorship of the Mishnah "Israel" does resonate as a differentiating category, with "not-Israel" (i.e., Gentile) the one routine antonym. Such a usage of "Israel" as a social entity very commonly occurs when someone wants for neutral purposes to distinguish Israelite from Gentile: thus, "If a majority is Israelite...; if a majority is Gentile..." (M. Mak. 2:5, 7). "Israelite" in contradistinction to "Gentile" occurs in such ways as these: "A Gentile who gave an Israelite..." (M. Hal. 3:5); "He who sells to a Gentile in the Land [of Israel] or to an Israelite outside of the Land..." (M. Sheb. 5:7); "He who receives a field from an Israelite, a Gentile, or a Samaritan..." (M. Dem. 6:1); "He who sells his field to a Gentile, and an Israelite went and bought it from him..." (M. Git. 4:9); "The ox of a Gentile that gored the ox of an Israelite..." and vice versa (M. B.Q. 4:3); "An Israelite women ['daughter'] should not serve as midwife to a Gentile..." (M. A.Z. 2:1); and so on throughout that tractate.

These usages treat the Gentile as one classification, an outsider, one not subject to the laws of the Torah (e.g., in connection with land ownership and the application of Seventh Year taboos), and the Israelite as another classification in that same connection. The statement of genealogical origin with an Israelite — not a Gentile — mother occurs at M. Bik. 1:4 and Qid. 4:7. At M. Ned. 3:11, "Gentile" is treated as the antonym of "Israelite": there it is said that "he who by vow prohibits himself from deriving benefit from an Israelite" may derive benefit from a Gentile. Along these same lines, "Israelite" as antonym for "Gentile" occurs at M. Git. 9:8, "What Israelites tell you..."; M. Mak. 2:5 (so too M. A.Z. 4:11), "A village in which Israelites and Gentiles dwell..."; and the like. The distinctions made in these usages, however, are not narrowly political. In many instances, the antonymic difference yields cultic results: for example, "A Gentile who separated heave-offering for produce belonging to an Israelite..." (M. Ter. 1:1). If on the Sabbath a Gentile performs an action for his own purposes, an Israelite may derive benefit from that action (M. Shab. 16:8; 23:4). What belongs to a Gentile is not subject to the prohibition of leaven on Passover (M. Pes. 2:3). "The uncircumcised" is taken to be a synonym for "Gentile," and "the circumcised" for the Israelite male. Thus if one takes a vow not to derive benefit from "the uncircumcised," the sense is understood not literally but figuratively: that is, circumcised Gentiles are included in the vow; uncircumcised Israelites are excluded from it. Certain descriptive statements distinguish "Israelite women" from "gentile women" (M. Nid. 2:1).

"We Israel" encompasses many "I's" — that is, individual Israelites (or Jews, a much less common usage). When the authorship of the Mishnah wishes to refer to an individual Jew, not surprisingly it speaks of "Israel," meaning an Israelite; occasionally, in context, this means "not a Gentile," but, commonly, it refers to a simple fact: it refers to an individual, one of "us" in general. As soon as we encounter "Israel" as the name of the group, we become aware of this further important sense of the name. The occurrences are typified by these statements: "An Israelite who married a *mamzer*-woman..." (M. Qid. 9:2); "He who undertakes to sharecrop a field belonging to an Israelite, a Gentile, a Samaritan..." (M. Dem. 6:1), meaning an individual person in the category of Israel, a Jew; "And let not a single soul of Israel be handed over to them" (M. Ter. 8:12), which has a similar sense; "People do not accept for share-cropping a field handed over on terms of 'iron flock' from an Israel[ite] [since it smacks of usury]" (M. B.M. 5:6); "Whoever saves..., whoever destroys a single life of Israel..." (M. San. 4:5), meaning, a Jew.

Another usage of "Israel" for an individual Jew occurs at M. Ned. 3:11 (and there are numerous equivalent passages): "Forbidden...that an Israelite derive benefit from me" means that benefit may be imparted to a non-Jew. Where the word "Israel" occurs in the plural, "Israelites," it always refers to two or more individual Jews: "Unless two Israelites prohibit one another..." (M. Er. 6:1); "In a city in which Gentiles and Israelites are located, it is permitted" (M. A.Z. 4:11). "Israel" may at times stand not for "a person of Jewish identity" but for "an Israelite, and not a priest," as at M. Yoma 6:3: "And he was an Israelite," but the difference and intent are readily determined in context. The usages in Tosefta and the later writings do not differ. "Israel" in the sense of an individual Jew, not in contradistinction to a Gentile, occurs at T. Dem. 7:6: "An Israelite who took a field for sharecropping from his fellow, intending to cut the grain..." This usage is as common in the Tosefta as in the Mishnah. Sifra knows Israel as both the people and any member of the people, and the same is so for the two Sifrés. In all, "Israel" as "we" marks off the insider from the outsider. But there is a second, quite contradictory, sense of the word, having nothing to do with inside and outside "Israel" at all.

We now once again reach the second of the two very common usages, namely, "Israel" as "not-priest," that is, Israel in contradistinction to *kohen* (priest), or, less commonly, to Levite. Israelite society was deemed divided into castes: priests, Levites, Israel, and on downward. "Israel" in the sense of the caste yields Israel as "common folk," always defined in contradistinction to Levites and *Kohanim* (priests). This usage occurs frequently, for example, Yoma 7:1: "For Israel unto itself..., for the priests unto themselves...." Israelites were permitted to enter the courtyard of the Temple, but the inner spaces were open only to priests; those places were closed to Israelites (see, e.g., M. Suk. 5:4). Related distinctions separated Israel from Nazirites; those who had taken the oath specified at Numbers 6; *mamzerim*; offspring of a couple that could never legally marry (M. M.S. 5:4); or other special cultic categories.

This usage is not difficult to distinguish from the other contrastive meaning of the word. Wherever we find "priest" or "Levite," the word "Israel" bears the sense of a distinct caste within the larger nation or people. A sample of such usage is as follows: "An Israelite who received from a priest or a Levite..." (M. Dem. 6:4.5); "The daughter of an Israelite who consumed food in the status of priestly rations and afterward married a priest..." (M. Ter. 6:2); and the like. The clause "The ox belonging to an Israelite that gored an ox belonging to the sanctuary" (M. B.Q. 4:3) is of the same order. In Kasovky's Mishnah concordance, two of nine columns of entries under "Israel" without further qualifying language are taken up with examples of this usage. Such a statement as "For they imposed upon themselves a strict rule, but an easy rule upon Israel" (M. Bes. 2:6; M. Ed.

3:10) treats "Israel" as the ordinary folk, in contradistinction to some higher caste or entity.

To be sure, the caste usage is not always pertinent. We find the contrast between "the court" and "all Israel" at M. R.H. 3:1. "Israel" as the people at large would then contrast to "the court." But "Israel" in the following clause means the entire nation: "So long as Israel looks upward, toward heaven..." (M. R.H. 3:8). Every usage of "Israel" in the sense of a particular group has a counterpart in "Israel" in the sense of a distinct caste within the group. Phrases and terms such as "and an Israelite," "to an Israelite," and "Israelites" all bear both senses; the concordance lists leave no doubt that the meanings are equally commonplace and mutually exclusive.

So who really is Israel? When we ask how the authorship of the Mishnah explicitly defined (an) "Israel," our attention is directed to the one passage in which that question is systematically answered (M. San. 11:1-2). It is framed, as a question of social definition must be, in terms of who is in and who is out. (An) "Israel" is defined within the categories of inclusion and exclusion: the ones who are in (implicitly) constitute the social entity or social group at hand; the others are out. When the Mishnah's authorship wishes to define "Israel" by itself and on its own terms, rather than as a classification among other classifications in an enormous system of taxonomy, "Israel" may be set forth not only as an entity in its own terms but also as sui generis. But, as we now expect, the context will be defined by supernatural considerations.

All Israelites — persons who hold the correct opinion — constitute Israel. On the subject of who is in and who is out there is no passage of the Mishnah and related literature more concrete and explicit than the one at hand. *But the "in" is not within this world at all.* Those who are "in" are those who enter or have a share of the world to come. Then all those Israelites who constitute in themselves the social entity, the group Israel, form a supernatural, not merely a social, entity — and no wonder all metaphors fail. The premise is that we speak only of Israel, and the result is the definition of Israel in terms we should not have anticipated at all: not Israel as against non-Israel/Gentile, nor Israel as against non-Israel/the priest, but Israel as against those who deny convictions now deemed — explicitly — indicatively and normatively to form the characteristics of Israel(ite). Here is an Israel that, at first glance, is defined not in relationships but intransitively and intrinsically. To state the result simply: Israel is implicitly sui generis. This becomes clear in the following:

A. All Israelites have a share in the world to come,

B. as it is said, "Your people also shall be all righteous; they shall inherit the land forever; the branch of my planting, the work of my hands, that I may be glorified" (Isa. 60:21).

C. And these are the ones who have no portion in the world to come:

D. He who says, the resurrection of the dead is a teaching which does not derive from the Torah, and the Torah does not come from Heaven; and an Epicurean.

E. R. Aqiba says, "Also: He who reads in heretical books,

F. "and he who whispers over a wound and says, 'I will put none of the diseases upon you which I have put on the Egyptians, for I am the Lord who heals you' (Exod. 15:26)."

G. Abba Saul says, "Also: He who pronounces the divine Name as it is spelled out." (M. San. 11:1)

Israel is defined inclusively: to be Israel is to have a share in the world to come. Israel then is a social entity that is made up of those who share a common conviction, and that Israel therefore bears an otherworldly destiny. Other social entities are not so defined within the Mishnah (and that by definition!), and it must follow that (an) Israel in the conception of the authorship of the Mishnah is sui generis, in that other social entities do not find their definition within the range of supernatural facts pertinent to Israel; (an) Israel is a social group that endows its individual members with life in the world to come; an Israel(ite) is one who enjoys the world to come. Excluded from this Israel are Israel(ite)s who within the established criteria of social identification exclude themselves. The power to define by relationships does not run out, however, since in this supernatural context of (an) Israel that is sui generis, we still know who is Israel because we are told who is "not-Israel," now, specific nonbelievers or sinners. These are, as we should expect, persons who reject the stated belief.

A. Three kings and four ordinary folk have no portion in the world to come.

B. Three kings: Jeroboam, Ahab, and Manasseh.

C. R. Judah says, "Manasseh has a portion in the world to come,

D. "since it is said, 'And he prayed to him and he was entreated of him and heard his supplication and brought him again to Jerusalem into his kingdom' (2 Chron. 33:13)."

E. They said to him, "To his kingdom he brought him back, but to the life of the world to come he did not bring him back."

F. Four ordinary folk: Balaam, Doeg, Ahitophel, and Gehazi. (M. San. 11:2)

Not only persons, but also classes of Israelites are specified, in all cases contributing to the definition of (an) Israel. The excluded classes of Israelites bear in common a supernatural fault, which is that they have sinned against God.

The catalogue of texts that follows begins with discussion of those excluded from the world to come who are not Israel, namely, the generation of the flood and the generation of the dispersion. This somewhat complicates matters because we should have thought that only (an) Israel was at issue in reference to enjoying the world to come. And if only (an) Israel was at issue, then Gentiles of whatever sort would hardly require specification. In other words, if the subject of the text at hand is the classes of excluded Israelites, who have sinned against God, then why include discussion of Gentiles? The answer is simply that the specified Gentiles are included because of their place in the biblical narrative. The focus of definition, thus, remains on Israel, pure and simple. This point is made clear in the second and third blocks of text below.

A. The generation of the flood has no share in the world to come,

B. and they shall not stand in the judgment,

C. since it is written, "My spirit shall not judge with man forever" (Gen. 6:3),

D. neither judgment nor spirit.

E. The generation of the dispersion has no share in the world to come,

F. since it is said, "So the Lord scattered them abroad from there upon the face of the whole earth" (Gen. 11:8).

G. "So the Lord scattered them abroad" — in this world.

H. "and the Lord scattered them from there" — in the world to come.

I. The men of Sodom have no portion in the world to come,

J. since it is said, "Now the men of Sodom were wicked and sinners against the Lord exceedingly" (Gen. 13:13).

K. "Wicked" — in this world.

L. "And sinners" — in the world to come.

M. But they will stand in judgment.

N. R. Nehemiah says, "Both these and those will not stand in judgment,

O. "for it is said, 'Therefore the wicked shall not stand in judgment [108A], nor sinners in the congregation of the righteous' (Ps. 1:5).

P. " 'Therefore the wicked shall not stand in judgment' — this refers to the generation of the flood.

Q. " 'Nor sinners in the congregation of the righteous' — this refers to the men of Sodom."

R. They said to him, "They will not stand in the congregation of the righteous, but they will stand in the congregation of the sinners."

S. The spies have no portion in the world to come,

T. as it is said, "Even those men who brought up an evil report of the land died by the plague before the Lord" (Num. 14:37).

U. "Died" — in this world.

V. "By the plague" — in the world to come.

W. "The generation of the wilderness has no portion in the world to come and will not stand in judgment,

X. "for it is written, 'In this wilderness they shall be consumed, and there they shall die' (Num. 14:35)." The words of R. Aqiba.

Y. R. Eliezer says, "Concerning them it says, 'Gather my saints together to me, those that have made a covenant with me by sacrifice' (Ps. 50:5)."

Z. "The party of Korah is not destined to rise up,

AA. "for it is written, 'And the earth closed upon them' — in this world.

BB. " 'And they perished from among the assembly' — in the world to come." The words of R. Aqiba.

CC. And R. Eliezer says, "Concerning them it says, 'The Lord kills and resurrects, brings down to Sheol and brings up again' (1 Sam. 2:6)." (M. San. 11:3A–CC)

DD. "The ten tribes are not destined to return,

EE. "since it is said, 'And he cast them into another land, as on this day' (Deut. 29:28). Just as the day passes and does not return, so they have gone their way and will not return." The words of R. Aqiba.

FF. R. Eliezer says, "Just as this day is dark and then grows light, so the ten tribes for whom it now is dark — thus in the future it is destined to grow light for them." (M. San. 11:3DD–FF)

A. The townsfolk of an apostate town have no portion in the world to come,

B. as it is said, "Certain base fellows [sons of Belial] have gone out from the midst of thee and have drawn away the inhabitants of their city" (Deut. 13:14).

C. And they are not put to death unless those who misled the [town] come from that same town and from that same tribe,

D. and unless the majority is misled,

E. and unless men did the misleading.

F. [If] women or children misled them,

G. or if a minority of the town was misled,

H. or if those who misled the town came from outside of it,

I. lo, they are treated as individuals [and not as a whole town],

J. and they [thus] require [testimony against them] by two witnesses, and a statement of warning, for each and every one of them.

K. This rule is more strict for individuals than for the community:

L. for individuals are put to death by stoning.

M. Therefore their property is saved.

N. But the community is put to death by the sword.

O. Therefore their property is lost. (M. San. 11:4–6)

The catalogue leaves us no doubt that the candidates for inclusion or exclusion are presented by the biblical narrative. Hence we see no implicit assumption that all *Gentiles* except those specified have a share in the world to come. That seems to me a proposition altogether beyond the imagination of our authorship. Tosefta Sanhedrin for its part does not suggest that some Gentiles enjoy the world to come.

A. The Israelites who sinned with their bodies and Gentiles who sinned with their bodies go down to Gehenna and are judged there for twelve months.

B. And after twelve months their souls perish, their bodies are burned, Gehenna absorbs them, and they are turned into dirt.

C. And the wind blows them and scatters them under the feet of the righteous,

D. as it is written, "And you shall tread down the wicked, for they shall be dust under the soles of the feet of the righteous in the day that I do this, says the Lord of Hosts" (Mal. 4:3). (T. San. 13:4A–D)

A. But heretics, apostates, traitors, Epicureans, those who deny the Torah, those who separate from the ways of the community, those who deny the resurrection of the dead, and whoever both sinned and caused the public to sin —

B. for example, Jeroboam and Ahab,

C. and those who sent their arrows against the land of the living and stretched out their hands against the "lofty habitation" [the Temple],

D. Gehenna is locked behind them, and they are judged therein for all generations,

E. since it is said, "And they shall go forth and look at the corpses of the men who were transgressors against me. For their worm dies not, and their fire is not quenched. And they shall be an abhorring unto all flesh" (Isa. 66:24).

F. Sheol will waste away, but they will not waste away,

G. for it is written, " ... and their form shall cause Sheol to waste away" (Ps. 49:14).

H. What made this happen to them? Because they stretched out their hand against the "lofty habitation,"

I. as it is said, "Because of his lofty habitation," and "lofty habitation" refers only to the Temple, as it is said, "I have surely built you as a lofty habitation, a place for you to dwell in forever" (1 Kings 8:13). (T. San. 13:5A–I)

The implicit principle of T. San. 13:5 is clearly that when it comes to the matters at hand, only Israelites, not Gentiles, are of concern. Accordingly, the authorship of the Tosefta seems to take for granted that Israel is a supernatural entity and that a person's separation from Israel is brought about by supernatural considerations. The upshot may be stated simply: when Israel is sui generis, it is because the context of definition speaks of supernatural and not this-worldly matters. When we come to the second phase of the unfolding of the writings of the Judaism of the dual Torah, we shall find a far more elaborate statement of the traits of that social entity that is sui generis. But the main point — that we deal with an entity that is supernatural and not subject to the rules of this world — defines matters throughout.

We turn to tractate Avot for a picture of two matters: first, meanings imputed to "Israel"; second, and much more interesting, where and how the category "Israel" plays a role in the comprehensive, systematic statement that is attempted by the authorship at hand. We find two pertinent sayings within the chains of tradition of tractate Avot, chapter 2. One refers to the government, an entity "out there," the other, to the community, treated in equally indeterminate terms. The point of the former is that governments are not to be trusted; the gist of the latter is that one is to preserve ties to the community:

2:3   [Judah, son of R. Judah the Patriarch:] "Be wary of the government, for they get friendly with a person only for their own convenience. They look like friends when it is to their benefit, but they do not stand by a person when he is in need."

2:4   ...Hillel says: "Do not walk out on the community." (Avot 2:3–4)

In neither saying do we find profound thought on the social entity Israel. What we have falls into the category of good advice on wise conduct, nothing more. "Israel" does not form a topic that receives sustained attention. Sayings that, from a systemic perspective, are equivalently neutral include the following:

> A. R. Hananiah, Prefect of the Priests, says, "Pray for the welfare of the government. For if it were not for fear of it, one man would swallow his fellow alive." (Avot 3:2A)

Again, sayings of this type do not contribute to a pattern of inquiry into the social entity Israel. They add up to good advice.

That is not to suggest that thought about the meaning of a social entity defined by shared traits and norms does not enter into the program of the document. Quite to the contrary: from a gathering of two persons on upward, the framers of Avot explicitly identify what they mean by a social entity and how they distinguish one such entity from another. But this entity they do not call (an) "Israel." They have another socially definitive category in mind:

3:2 B. R. Hananiah b. Teradion says, "[If] two sit together and between them do not pass teachings of the Torah, lo, this is a seat of the scornful, as it is said, 'Nor sits in the seat of the scornful' (Ps. 1:1).

"But two who are sitting, and words of the Torah do pass between them — the Presence is with them, as it is said, 'Then they that feared the Lord spoke with one another, and the Lord hearkened and heard, and a book of remembrance was written before him, for them that feared the Lord and gave thought to his name' (Mal. 3:16).

"I know that this applies to two. How do I know that even if a single person sits and works on the Torah, the Holy One, blessed be He, set aside a reward for him? As it is said, 'Let him sit alone and keep silent, because he has laid it upon him' (Lam. 3:28)." (Avot 3:2B)

3:3   R. Simeon says, "Three who ate at a single table and did not talk about teachings of the Torah while at that table are as though they ate from dead sacrifices (Ps. 106:28), as it is said, 'For all tables are full of vomit and filthiness [if they are] without God' (Ps. 106:28).

"But three who ate at a single table and did talk about teachings of the Torah while at that table are as if they ate at the table of the Omnipresent, blessed is he, as it is said, 'And he said to me, This is the table that is before the Lord' (Ezra. 41:22)." (Avot 3:3)

3:6   R. Halafta of Kefar Hananiah says, "Among ten who sit and work hard on the Torah the Presence comes to rest, as it is said, 'God stands in the congregation of God' (Ps. 82:1).

"And how do we now that the same is so even of five? For it is said, 'And he has founded his group upon the earth' (Amos 9:6).

"And how do we know that this is so even of three? Since it is said, 'And he judges among the judges' (Ps. 82:1).

"And how do we know that this is so even of two? Because it is said, 'Then they that feared the Lord spoke with one another, and the Lord hearkened and heard' (Mal. 3:16).

"And how do we know that this is so even of one? Since it is said, 'In every place where I record my name I will come to you and I will bless you' (Exod. 20:24)." (Avot 3:6)

The concluding saying, concerning "even...one," alerts us to the fact that our definitions correspond to those in M. San. 10:1ff. "Israel" is made up of "Israelites" — even one individual constituting an Israel when such a person engages in Torah study. A social entity takes shape in one of two ways: either because people do exchange Torah teachings or because they do not do so. Along these same lines, the individual and Israel serve as examples of the same thing, namely, God's love, which is all the greater because the person and the social entity are informed of that love. Like Israel in the Mishnah, here too Israel is inert, not generating a proposition but contributing to the statement of one. The proposition has to do with God's love, illustrated, by the way, in the condition of Israel too:

A. He would say, "Precious is the human being, who was created in the image [of God]. It was an act of still greater love that it was made known to him that he was created in the image [of God], as it is said, 'For in the image of God he made man' (Gen. 9:6)."

B. Precious is Israel [that is, are Israelites], who are called children to the Omnipresent. It was an act of still greater love that it was made known to them that they were called children to the Omnipresent, as it is said, "You are the children of the Lord your God" (Deut. 14:1).

C. Precious are Israelites, to whom was given the precious thing. It was an act of still greater love that it was made known to them that to them was given that precious thing with which the world was made, as it is said, "For I give you a good doctrine. Do not forsake my Torah" (Prov. 4:2). (Avot 3:14)

Once more we observe an Israel that is sui generis, beginning with a simple fact. "Israel" here means "Israelite," not the social entity viewed as a collectivity, but those who belong to the entity — and therefore constitute that entity, even one by one. These are the children of the Lord, as Scripture says; Israel(ites) are shown to be beloved because the Torah was given to them and because that fact was made known to them. The central issue in all these statements is the Torah, not Israel. What is celebrated is the gift of the Torah. So in the theology of Judaism, Israel is Israel by virtue of the Torah.

3

Israel as Family:
The Body of Faith

The profound shift in the characterization of Israel that took place in the late fourth- and fifth-century documents responded to the crisis presented by the political triumph of Christianity. Now "Israel" found definition on its own terms, not principally in relationship to "non-Israel," whatever that, in context, may have meant. "Israel" now bore an absolute, not a relative, meaning, with concrete, not abstract, valence. That autonomy was sometimes expressed by means of comparison, but comparison did not define Israel. The documents that carried forward and continued the Mishnah exhibit striking changes, in particular within those writings brought to closure at the end of the fourth century and in the hundred years thereafter, and the representation of Israel followed suit. These writings, over all, present a Judaic system interested in sanctification in the here and now and also in salvation at the end of time, a system in which the teleology bore in its wake an eschatological doctrine of a salvific character.

When sages at the end of the fourth century wished to know what (an) Israel was, they reread the scriptural story of Israel's origins. Scripture told them the story of a man who had two names: first he was called Jacob, and then, after wrestling with the angel, he was called Israel. The children of this man were thus both "the children of Jacob" and "the children of Israel." By extension, Israel formed the family of Abraham and Sarah; Isaac and Rebecca; and Jacob, Leah, and Rachel. "Israel" therefore invoked the theory of genealogy to explain the bonds that linked persons unseen into a single social entity; the shared traits were imputed, not empirical. That social theory of Israel — a simple one, really, and easily grasped — bore consequences in two ways.

First, children in general were admonished to follow the good example of their parents. The deeds of the patriarchs and matriarchs were taught as examples of how the children were to act. Second — and of greater interest in an account of Israel as a social theory — Israel lived twice, once in the patriarchs and matriarchs, a second time in the lives of the descendants who relived those earlier lives. The stories of the formative family were carefully reread to provide a picture of the meaning of the events in the lives of the latter-day descendants of that same family. Accordingly, the lives of the patriarchs signaled the history of Israel.

The polemical purpose of the claim that the abstraction "Israel" was to be compared to the family of the mythic ancestor lies right at the surface. With another Israel, the Christian Church, now claiming to constitute the true one, Jews found it possible to confront that claim and to turn it against the other side: "You claim to form 'Israel after the spirit.' Fine, and *we* are Israel after the flesh — and genealogy forms the link, that alone." (Converts to Judaism did not present an anomaly because they were held to be children of Abraham and Sarah, who had "made souls," that is, converts, in Haran, a point repeated in the documents of the period.) That fleshly continuity formed all of "us" into a single family, rendering spurious the notion that Israel could be other than genealogically defined. But that polemic is adventitious and not primary, for the theory provided a quite separate component to those sages' larger system.

The theology of Israel as family supplied an encompassing theory of society, accounting for that sense of constituting a corporate social entity that clearly infused the documents of the Judaism of the dual Torah from the very outset. Such a theory explained not only who Israel as a whole was. It also set forth the responsibilities of Israel's social entity, its society; it defined the character of that entity; it explained who owes what to whom and why; and it accounted for the inner structure and interplay of relationship within the community, here and now, constituted by Jews in their villages and neighborhoods of towns. Accordingly, Israel as family bridged the gap between an account of the entirety of the social group Israel and a picture of the components of that social group as they lived out their lives in their households and villages. An encompassing theory of society, covering all components from least to greatest, holding the whole together in correct order and proportion, derived from Israel viewed as extended family.

The Mishnah could explain a village and "all Israel," just as its system used the word "Israel" for the individual and the entire social entity. But the region and its counterparts; the "we" composed of regions; the corporate society of the Jews of a given country, language-group, and the like; the real-life world of communities — these did not constitute subdivisions of the Israel that knew all and each but nothing in between. The omitted entity was the family itself, which played no important role in the Mishnah's system, except as one of the taxonomic indicators. By contrast, Israel as family imparted to the details an autonomy and a meaning of their own, *so that each complex component of the whole formed a microcosm of the whole: from family to village to Israel as one large family.*

The village then comprised Israel as much as did the region, the neighborhood, the corporate society people could empirically identify, and the theoretical social entity they could only imagine. All formed "all Israel," viewed under the aspect of heaven, and, of still greater consequence, each household — that is, each building block of the village community — constituted in itself a model of, the model for, Israel. The utter abstraction of the Mishnah had left Israel, as individual or as "all Israel," without articulated linkage to the concrete middle range of the Jews' everyday social life. Dealing with exquisite detail and the intangible whole, the Mishnah's system had left that realm of the society of Jews in the workaday household and village outside the metaphorical frame of Israel, and Israel viewed in the image of, after the likeness of, family made up that omitted middle range.

That theory of Israel as a society made up of persons who because they constituted a family stood in a clear relationship of obligation and responsibility to one another corresponded to what people much later would call the social contract, a kind of compact that in palpable ways told families and households how in the aggregate they formed something larger and tangible. The web of interaction that had once been spun out of concrete interchange was now spun out of not the gossamer thread of abstraction and theory but the tough hemp of family ties. Israel formed a society because Israel was compared to an extended family. That, in sum and substance, supplied to the Jews in their households (themselves a made-up category that, in the end, transformed the relationship of the nuclear family into an abstraction capable of holding together quite unrelated persons) an account of the tie from household to household, from village to village, encompassing ultimately "all Israel."

If "we" form a family, then we know full well what links us — the common ancestry, the obligations imposed by common ancestry upon the cousins who make up the family today. The link between, on the one hand, the commonplace interactions and relationships that make "us" into a community and, on the other hand, that encompassing entity Israel or "all Israel" now is drawn. The large comprehends the little: the abstraction of "us" overall ("the circumcised," for instance) gains concrete reality in the "us" of the here and now of home and village, all together, all forming a "family." In that fundamental way, the theology of Israel as family therefore provided the field-theory of Israel that linked the most abstract component, the entirety of the social group, to the most mundane, the specificity of the household. One theory, framed in that theology of such surpassing simplicity, now held the whole together. The theology of family provided an encompassing theory of society, an account of the social contract encompassing all social entities, Jews and Gentiles as well.

In what follows we shall survey how Israel as family comes to expression in the document that makes the most sustained and systematic statement of the matter, Genesis Rabbah. In this theory we should not miss the extraordinary polemic utility, of which, in passing, we have already taken note. Israel as family also understood itself to form a nation or people. As we shall presently see, that nation-people held a land, a rather peculiar, enchanted, or holy land, one that, in its imputed traits, was as sui generis as Israel was in the metaphorical thought of the system at hand. In competing for this land, Israel laid claim to it by calling it the Land of Israel. That claim rested on a right of inheritance such as a family enjoys, and this was made explicit. The following passage shows how high the stakes were in the claim to constitute the genealogical descendant of the ancestors:

1. A. "But to the sons of his concubines, Abraham gave gifts, and while he was still living, he sent them away from his son Isaac, eastward to the east country" (Gen. 25:6).

   B. In the time of Alexander of Macedonia the sons of Ishmael came to dispute with Israel about the birthright, and with them came two wicked families, the Canaanites and the Egyptians.

   C. They said, "Who will go and engage in a disputation with them?"

   D. Gebiah b. Qosem [the enchanter] said, "I shall go and engage in a disputation with them."

   E. They said to him, "Be careful not to let the Land of Israel fall into their possession."

   F. He said to them, "I shall go and engage in a disputation with them. If I win over them, well and good. And if not, you may say, 'Who is this hunchback to represent us?' "

   G. He went and engaged in a disputation with them. Said to them Alexander of Macedonia, "Who lays claim against whom?"

   H. The Ishmaelites said, "We lay claim, and we bring our evidence from their own Torah: 'But he shall acknowledge the firstborn, the son of the hated' (Deut. 21:17). Now Ishmael was the firstborn. [We therefore claim the land as heirs of the firstborn of Abraham.]"

   I. Said to him Gebiah b. Qosem, "My royal lord, does a man not do whatever he likes with his sons?"

   J. He said to him, "Indeed so."

   K. "And lo, it is written, 'Abraham gave all that he had to Isaac' (Gen. 25:2)."

L. [Alexander asked,] "Then where is the deed of gift to the other sons?"

M. He said to him, " 'But to the sons of his concubines, Abraham gave gifts, [and while he was still living, he sent them away from his son Isaac, eastward to the east country]' (Gen. 25:6)."

N. [The Ishmaelites had no claim on the land.] They abandoned the field in shame. (Gen. Rab. 61:7)

In the following text, the metaphor shifts. The notion of Israel today as the family of Abraham, as against the Ishmaelites, also of the same family, gives way. But the theme of family records persists. Canaan has no claim, for Canaan was also a family, comparable to Israel — but descended from a slave. The power of the theology of family is that it can explain not only the social entity formed by Jews but the social entities confronted by them. All fell into the same genus, making up diverse species. The theory of society before us — that is, the theory of Israel — thus accounts for the existence, also, of all societies, and, as we shall see when we deal with Rome, the theory of Israel does so with extraordinary force.

O. The Canaanites said, "We lay claim, and we bring our evidence from their own Torah. Throughout their Torah it is written, 'the land of Canaan.' So let them give us back our land."

P. Said to him Gebiah b. Qosem, "My royal lord, does a man not do whatever he likes with his slave?"

Q. He said to him, "Indeed so."

R. He said to him, "And lo, it is written, 'A slave of slaves shall Canaan be to his brothers' (Gen. 9:25). So they are really our slaves."

S. [The Canaanites had no claim to the land and in fact should be serving Israel.] They abandoned the field in shame. (Gen. Rab. 61:7)

The same theology serves both "Israel" and "Canaan." Each formed the latter-day heir of the earliest family, and both lived out the original paradigm. The mode of thought at hand imputes the same genus to both social entities and then makes it possible to distinguish among the two species. We shall see the same mode of thought — the family, then the designation of which wing of the family — when we consider the confrontation with Christianity and with Rome, in each case conceived in the same personal way. The theology applies to both and yields its own meanings for each. The final claim in the passage below moves away from the theology of family. But the notion of a continuous, physical descent is implicit here as well. Israel has inherited the wealth of Egypt, and the notion of inheritance forms a component of the theology of family.

> T. The Egyptians said, "We lay claim, and we bring our evidence from their own Torah. Six hundred thousand of them left us, taking away our silver and gold utensils: 'They despoiled the Egyptians' (Exod. 12:36). Let them give them back to us."

> U. Gebiah b. Qosem said, "My royal lord, six hundred thousand men worked for them for two hundred and ten years, some as silversmiths and some as goldsmiths. Let them pay us our salary at the rate of a *denar* a day."

> V. The mathematicians went and added up what was owing, and they had not reached the sum covering a century before the Egyptians had to forfeit what they had claimed. They abandoned the field in shame.

> W. [Alexander] wanted to go up to Jerusalem. The Samaritans said to him, "Be careful. They will not permit you to enter their most holy sanctuary."

> X. When Gebiah b. Qosem found out about this, he went and made for himself two felt shoes, with two precious stones worth twenty-thousand pieces of silver set in them. When he got to the mountain of the house [of the Temple], he said to him, "My royal lord, take off your shoes and put on these two felt slippers, for the floor is slippery, and you should not slip and fall."

> Y. When they came to the most holy sanctuary, he said to him, "Up to this point, we have the right to enter. From this point onward, we do not have the right to enter."

> Z. He said to him, "When we get out of here, I'm going to even out your hump."

AA. He said to him, "You will be called a great surgeon and get a big fee." (Gen. Rab. 61:7)

The Ishmaelites, Abraham's children, deprived as they were of their inheritance, fall into the same genus as does Israel. So too did Canaan. As to the Egyptians, that is a different matter. Now Israel is that same Israel of which Scripture spoke. The social metaphor shifts within the story though, of course, the story is not affected.

Families inherited the estate of the founders, and Israel was a family with a sizable heritage and inheritance. Thinking concretely rather than abstractly, sages personalized these relations through the invented personalities, though they were also able to make perfectly clear statements for themselves. Along these same lines, when the Church theologians-historians faced the task of explaining the connection between diverse nations or peoples and the Church, they worked out relationships between the king of a country and Jesus, as in the case of the correspondence between Jesus and Abgar, which accounted for the place of the church of Edessa within the family of Christianity. Since the Church understood that not only Jesus' blood relatives but also his disciples, standing in a supernatural relationship with him, entered into the original communion, the invented discipleship of kings made a place, within a larger social theory of the Church, for the new and diverse groups. When, in the fourth century, a principal world ruler did convert, the Church had an understanding of the role of persons and personalities in the history of salvation. The mode of thought before us, therefore, finds ample place in a larger scheme of thinking about society and the relationships of its components.

Families have histories, and Israel as family found in the record of its family history those points of coherence that transformed events into meaningful patterns, that is, the history of the social unit, the nation-family, as a whole. This matter is simply expressed in common sayings: "Like parent, like child"; "The apple does not fall far from the tree"; and the like. Whether true or false, that folk wisdom surely accounts for the commonsense quality of sages' search, in the deeds of the patriarchs and matriarchs, for messages concerning the future history of the children. But sages assuredly were not common folk. They were philosophers, and their inquiry constituted a chapter in the history of what used to be called natural philosophy, and what today we know as social science. Specifically, sages looked in the facts of history for the laws of history. They proposed to generalize and, out of generalization, to explain their own particular circumstance. That is why we may compare them to social scientists or social philosophers, trying to turn anecdotes into insight and to demonstrate how we may know the difference between impressions and truths. Genesis provided facts concerning the family. Careful sifting of those facts would yield the laws that dictated why to that family things happened one way rather than some other.

Among these social laws of the family history, one took priority, the law that explained the movement of empires upward and downward and pointed toward the ultimate end of it all. Scripture provided the model for the ages of empires, yielding a picture of four monarchies, to be followed by Israel as the fifth. Sages repeated this familiar viewpoint (one we shall rehearse when we consider Israel as sui generis, now for quite other reasons). In reading Genesis, in particular, they found that time and again events in the lives of the patriarchs prefigured the four monarchies, among which, of course, the fourth, last, and most intolerable was Rome. Israel's history falls under God's dominion. Whatever will happen carries out God's plan, and that plan for the future has been laid out in the account of the origins supplied by Genesis. The fourth kingdom, Rome, is part of that plan, which we can discover by carefully studying Abraham's life and God's word to him.

1. A. "Then the Lord said to Abram, 'Know of a surety [that your descendants will be sojourners in a land that is not theirs, and they will be slaves there, and they will be oppressed for four hundred years; but I will bring judgment on the nation which they serve, and afterward they shall come out with great possessions]'" (Gen. 15:13–14):

    B. "Know" that I shall scatter them.

    C. "Of a certainty" that I shall bring them back together again.

D. "Know" that I shall put them out as a pledge [in expiation of their sins].

E. "Of a certainty" that I shall redeem them.

F. "Know" that I shall make them slaves.

G. "Of a certainty" that I shall free them. (Gen. Rab. 44:18)

Number 1 parses the cited verse and joins within its simple formula the entire history of Israel, punishment and forgiveness alike. Not only the patriarchs but also the matriarchs so acted as to shape the future life of the family, Israel. One extended statement of the matter suffices. The next citation refers to how sages take up the detail of Abraham's provision of a bit of water, showing what that act had to do with the history of Israel later on. The intricate working out of the whole then encompasses the merit of the patriarchs, the way in which the deeds of the patriarchs provide a sign for proper conduct for their children and for the history and salvation of Israel.

2.   A. "Let a little water be brought" (Gen. 18:4):

B. Said to him the Holy One, blessed be he, "You have said, 'Let a little water be brought' (Gen. 18:4). By your life, I shall pay your descendants back for this: 'Then sang Israel this song, "Spring up O well, sing you to it" ' (Num. 21:7)."

C. That recompense took place in the wilderness. Where do we find that it took place in the Land of Israel as well?

D. "A land of brooks of water" (Deut. 8:7).

E. And where do we find that it will take place in the age to come?

F. "And it shall come to pass in that day that living waters shall go out of Jerusalem" (Zech. 14:8).

G. ["And wash your feet" (Gen. 18:4)]: [Said to him the Holy One, blessed be he,] "You have said, 'And wash your feet.' By your life, I shall pay your descendants back for this: 'Then I washed you in water' (Ezra. 16:9)."

H. That recompense took place in the wilderness. Where do we find that it took place in the Land of Israel as well?

I. "Wash you, make you clean" (Isa. 1:16).

J. And where do we find that it will take place in the age to come?

K. "When the Lord will have washed away the filth of the daughters of Zion" (Isa. 4:4).

L. [Said to him the Holy One, blessed be he,] "You have said, 'And rest yourselves under the tree' (Gen. 18:4). By your life, I shall pay your descendants back for this: 'He spread a cloud for a screen' (Ps. 105:39)."

M. That recompense took place in the wilderness. Where do we find that it took place in the Land of Israel as well?

N. "You shall dwell in booths for seven days" (Lev. 23:42).

O. And where do we find that it will take place in the age to come?

P. "And there shall be a pavilion for a shadow in the day-time from the heat" (Isa. 4:6).

Q. [Said to him the Holy One, blessed be he,] "You have said, 'While I fetch a morsel of bread that you may refresh yourself' (Gen. 18:5). By your life, I shall pay your descendants back for this: 'Behold I will cause to rain bread from heaven for you' (Exod. 16:45)."

R. That recompense took place in the wilderness. Where do we find that it took place in the Land of Israel as well?

S. "A land of wheat and barley" (Deut. 8:8).

T. And where do we find that it will take place in the age to come?

U. "He will be as a rich grain field in the land" (Ps. 82:16).

V. [Said to him the Holy One, blessed be he,] "You ran after the herd ['And Abraham ran to the herd' (Gen. 18:7)]. By your life, I shall pay your descendants back for this: 'And there went forth a wind from the Lord and brought across quails from the sea' (Num. 11:27)."

W. That recompense took place in the wilderness. Where do we find that it took place in the Land of Israel as well?

X. "Now the children of Reuben and the children of Gad had a very great multitude of cattle" (Num. 32:1).

Y. And where do we find that it will take place in the age to come?

Z. "And it will come to pass in that day that a man shall rear a young cow and two sheep" (Isa. 7:21).

AA. [Said to him the Holy One, blessed be he,] "You stood by them: 'And he stood by them under the tree while they ate' (Gen. 18:8). By your life, I shall pay your descendants back for this: 'And the Lord went before them' (Exod. 13:21)."

BB. That recompense took place in the wilderness. Where do we find that it took place in the Land of Israel as well?

CC. "God stands in the congregation of God" (Ps. 82:1).

DD. And where do we find that it will take place in the age to come?

EE. "The breaker is gone up before them...and the Lord at the head of them" (Mic. 2:13). (Gen. Rab. 48:10)

Everything that Abraham did brought a reward to his descendants. The enormous emphasis on the way in which Abraham's deeds prefigured the history of Israel, both in the wilderness and in the Land and, finally, in the age to come, provokes us to wonder who held that there were other children of Abraham beside this Israel. The answer is clear: the triumphant Christians in particular, who right from the beginning, with Paul and the evangelists, imputed that status to the earliest generations and said it in so many words. We note that there are five statements of the same proposition, each drawing upon a clause in the base verse. The extended statement moreover serves as a sustained introduction to the treatment of the individual clauses that now follow, item by item. Obviously, it is the merit of the ancestors that connects the living Israel to the lives of the patriarchs and matriarchs of old.

While Abraham founded Israel, Isaac and Jacob carried forth the birthright and the blessing. This they did through the process of selection, ending in the assignment of the birthright to Jacob alone. The importance of that fact for the definition of "Israel" hardly requires explication. The lives of all three patriarchs flowed together, each being identified with the others as a single long life. This immediately produced the proposition that the historical life of Israel, the nation, continued the individual lives of the patriarchs. The theory of who is Israel, therefore, is seen once more to have rested on genealogy: Israel is one extended family, all being children of the same fathers and mothers, the patriarchs and matriarchs of Genesis. This theory of Israelite society, and of the Jewish people in the time of the sages of Genesis Rabbah, made the people a family and made genealogy a kind of ecclesiology. The importance of that proposition in countering the Christian claim to be a new Israel cannot escape notice. Israel, sages maintained, is Israel after the flesh, and that in a most literal sense. But the basic claim, for its part, depended upon the facts of Scripture, not upon the logical requirements of theological dispute. Here is how those facts emerged in the case of Isaac:

1. A. "These are the descendants of Isaac, Abraham's son: Abraham was the father of Isaac" (Gen. 25:19):

   B. Abram was called Abraham: "Abram, the same is Abraham" (1 Chron. 1:27).

   C. Isaac was called Abraham: "These are the descendants of Isaac, Abraham's son, Abraham."

   D. Jacob was called Israel, as it is written, "Your name shall be called no more Jacob but Israel" (Gen. 32:29).

   E. Isaac also was called Israel: "And these are the names of the children of Israel, who came into Egypt, Jacob and his sons" (Gen. 46:8).

   F. Abraham was called Israel as well.

   G. R. Nathan said, "This matter is deep: 'Now the time that the children of Israel dwelt in Egypt' (Exod. 12:40), and in the land of Canaan and in the land of Goshen, 'was four hundred and thirty years' (Exod. 12:40)." [Freedman (*Genesis*, Midrash Rabbah, ed. H. Freedman and M. Simon [New York: Soncino, 1983], p. 557, n. 6): They were in Egypt for only 210 years. Hence their sojourn in Canaan and Goshen must be added, which means, from the birth of Isaac. Hence the children of Israel commence with Isaac. And since he was Abraham's son, it follows that Abraham was called Israel.] (Gen. Rab. 63:3)

The polemic at hand, linking the patriarchs to the history of Israel, claiming that all of the patriarchs bear the same names, derives proof, in part, from the base verse. But the composition in no way rests upon the exegesis of the base verse. Its syllogism transcends the case at hand. The importance of Isaac in particular derived from his relationship to the two nations that would engage in struggle, Jacob, who was and is Israel, and Esau, who stood for Rome. By himself, as a symbol for Israel's history, Isaac remains a shadowy figure. Still, Isaac plays his role in setting forth the laws of Israel's history. To understand what is to follow, we recall that Esau, in sages' typology, always stands for Rome. Later we shall see that the representation of Esau as brother and enemy distinguishes Esau/Rome from all other nations. Esau is not an outsider, not a Gentile, but also not Israel, legitimate heir. We once more recall the power of the social theory to hold together all of the middle-range components of society: all nations within a single theory. The genealogical theology in the next citation displays that remarkable capacity:

1.   A.   "[He said, 'Behold I am old; I do not know the day of my death.] Now then take your weapons, [your quiver and your bow, and go out to the field and hunt game for me, and prepare for me savory food, such as I love, and bring it to me that I may eat; that I may bless you before I die']" (Gen. 27:2–4):

     B.   "Sharpen your hunting gear, so that you will not feed me carrion or an animal that was improperly slaughtered.

     C.   "Take your *own* hunting gear, so that you will not feed me meat that has been stolen or grabbed." (Gen. Rab. 65:13)

Isaac's first point is that Esau does not ordinarily observe the food laws, for example, concerning humane slaughter of animals. He furthermore steals, while, by inference, Jacob takes only what he has lawfully acquired. This prepares the way for the main point:

2.   A.   "Your quiver":

     B.   [Since the word for "quiver" and the word for "held in suspense" share the same consonants, we interpret the statement as follows:] he said to him, "Lo, the blessings [that I am about to give] are held in suspense. For the one who is worthy of a blessing, there will be a blessing."

3. A. Another matter: "Now then take your weapons, your quiver and your bow and go out to the field":

    B. "Weapons" refers to Babylonia, as it is said, "And the weapons he brought to the treasure house of his god" (Gen. 2:2).

    C. "Your quiver" speaks of Media, as it says, "So they suspended Haman on the gallows" (Esther 7:10). [The play on the words is the same as at no. 2.]

    D. "And your bow" addresses Greece: "For I bend Judah for me, I fill the bow with Ephraim, and I will store up your sons, O Zion, against your sons, O Javan [Greece]" (Zech. 9:13).

    E. "And go out to the field" means Edom: "Unto the land of Seir, the field of Edom" (Gen. 32:4). (Gen. Rab. 65:13)

Once more the patriarchs lay out the future history of their family and, in dealing with their own affairs, prefigure what is to come. The power of the theology of family is not exhausted in its capacity to link household to household; quite to the contrary, as with any really successful theology, it draws everything into one thing and makes sense of the whole all together and all at once. Here the households that are joined are today's and yesterday's and those of the entirety of past and future.

5. A. "And Rebecca was listening when Isaac spoke to his son Esau. So when Esau went to the field to hunt for game and bring it . . . " (Gen. 27:5):

    B. If he found it, well and good.

    C. And if not, " . . . to bring it" even by theft or violence. (Gen. Rab. 65:13)

The matter of the blessing is represented as more conditional than the narrative suggests. Isaac now is not sure who will get the blessing; his sense is that it will go to whoever deserves it. Number 3 (see above) moves from the moral to the national, making the statement a clear reference to the history of Israel (as though, by this point, it were not obvious). What the author of number 5 contributes, then, is the specific details. The compositor moves the reader's mind from the philological to the moral to the national dimension of the exegesis of the statements at hand. Esau steals, but Jacob takes only what is lawful.

Jacob's contribution to knowledge of the meaning and end of Israel's history, as sages uncovered it, is exemplified in the following:

1. A. "...so that I come again to my father's house in peace, then the Lord shall be my God" (Gen. 28:20–22):

    B. R. Joshua of Sikhnin in the name of R. Levi: "The Holy One, blessed be he, took the language used by the patriarchs and turned it into a key to the redemption of their descendants.

    C. "Said the Holy One, blessed be he, to Jacob, 'You have said, "Then the Lord shall be my God." By your life, all of the acts of goodness, blessing, and consolation which I am going to carry out for your descendants I shall bestow only by using the same language:

    D. " ' "Then, in that day, living waters shall go out from Jerusalem" (Zech. 14:8). "Then, in that day, a man shall rear a young cow and two sheep" (Isa. 7:21). "Then, in that day, the Lord will set his hand again the second time to recover the remnant of his people" (Isa. 11:11). "Then, in that day, the mountains shall drop down sweet wine" (Joel 4:18). "Then, in that day, a great horn shall be blown and they shall come who were lost in the land of Assyria" (Isa. 27:13).' " (Gen. Rab. 70:6)

The union of Jacob's biography and Israel's history yields the above passage. It is important only because it says once again what we have now heard throughout our survey of Genesis Rabbah — but it makes the statement as explicit as one can imagine. Now the history of the redemption of Israel is located in the colloquy between Jacob and Laban's sons:

1. A. "Now Laban had two daughters, the name of the older was Leah, and the name of the younger was Rachel" (Gen. 29:16):

    B. They were like two beams running from one end of the world to the other.

    C. This one produced captains and that one produced captains, this one produced kings and that one produced kings, this one produced lion tamers and that one produced lion tamers, this one produced conquerors of nations and that one produced conquerors of nations, this one produced those who divided countries and that one produced dividers of countries.

D. The offering brought by the son of this one overrode the prohibitions of the Sabbath, and the offering brought by the son of that one overrode the prohibitions of the Sabbath.

E. The war fought by this one overrode the prohibitions of the Sabbath, and the war fought by that one overrode the prohibitions of the Sabbath.

F. To this one were given two nights, and to that one were given two nights.

G. The night of Pharaoh and the night of Sennacherib were for Leah, and the night of Gideon was for Rachel, and the night of Mordecai was for Rachel, as it is said, "On that night the king could not sleep" (Esther 6:1). (Gen. Rab. 70:15)

The theology encompasses not only Israel but also Rome, to which we shall turn in the next chapter. It makes sense of all the important social entities, for in this theology, Israel is consubstantial with other social entities, which relate to Israel just as Israel as a society relates to itself, present and past. Transitive comparison only vindicates Israel as sui generis. Accordingly, Rome is a family just as "Israel" is, and, more to the point, Rome enters into Israel's life in an intelligible way precisely because Rome too is a part of that same family that is constituted by Israel. That is a stunning claim, working itself out time after time so smoothly, with such self-evidence, as to conceal its daring. Again we see how the theology that joins past to present, household to household to "all Israel," in fact encompasses the other noteworthy social entity and takes it into full account — a powerful, successful field-theory indeed. "Non-Israel" accommodates and classifies, but it does not explain.

Once sages had defined the social entity of Israel by analogy with a family, they naturally imposed upon social entities round about the same metaphor, which, in its nature, is inclusive and not exclusive. That instrument of thought therefore allowed sages to explain within a single, unitary theory what happened to both Israel and everyone else that mattered. If, in Genesis Rabbah, Abraham, Isaac, and Jacob stand for Israel later on, then Ishmael, Edom, and Esau represent Rome. Hence whatever sages find out about those figures tells them something about Rome and its character, history, and destiny. God has un-conditionally promised to redeem Israel, but if Israel repents, then the redemption will come with greater glory. Here, in the context of that conviction, is Ishmael's lesson:

3. A. ["He shall be a wild ass of a man, [his hand against every man and every man's hand against him, and he shall dwell over against all his kinsmen]...his hand against every man and every man's hand against him" (Gen. 16:12)]: Said R. Eleazar, "When is it the case that 'his hand is against every man and every man's hand against him'?

   B. "When he comes concerning whom it is written: 'And where-soever the children of men, the beasts of the field, and the fowl of the heaven dwell, has he given them into your hand' (Dan. 2:38). [Freedman (*Genesis*, Midrash Rabbah, vol. 1, p. 386, n. 2): In the days of Nebuchadnezzar, whose ruthless policy of conquest aroused the whole world against him.]

   C. "That is in line with the following verse of Scripture: 'Of Kedar and of the kingdoms of Hazor, which Nebuchadnez-zar smote' (Jer. 49:28). His name is spelled 'Nebuchadnezzar' because he shut them up in the wilderness and killed them." [Freedman (*Genesis*, Midrash Rabbah, vol. 1, p. 386, n. 4): A play on the name, which, with the present spelling, ends in *asar*, spelled with an *alef*, as though it were *asar*, spelled with an *ayin* and yielding the meaning, shut up.]

4. A. ["...and he shall dwell over against all his kinsmen]" (Gen. 16:12):

   B. Here the word-choice is "dwell" while later on it is "he fell" (Gen. 25:18).

   C. So long as Abraham was alive, "he [Ishmael] shall dwell." Once he died, "he fell." [His father's merit no longer pro-tected him.]

   D. Before he laid hands on the Temple, "he shall dwell." After he laid hands on the Temple, "he fell."

   E. In this world, "he shall dwell." In the world to come, "he fell." (Gen. Rab. 45:9)

Numbers 3 and 4 move from the figure of Ishmael to those like him: Nebuchadnezzar, then Rome. The Temple was de-stroyed by each of these persons, in the tradition of Ishmael.

The conclusion then provides the hope to Israel that the enemy will perish, at least in the world to come. So the passage is read both as a literal statement and also as an effort to prefigure the history of Israel's suffering and redemption. Ishmael, standing now for Christian Rome, claims God's blessing, but Isaac gets it, as Jacob will take it from Esau. The following works the contrast of Ishmael as against Isaac, yielding the same polemic against Rome:

1. A. "God said, 'No, but Sarah your wife [shall bear you a son, and you shall call his name Isaac. I will establish my covenant with him as an everlasting covenant for his descendants after him.] As for Ishmael, I have heard you. Behold, I will bless him and make him fruitful and multiply him exceedingly. He shall be the father of twelve princes, and I will make him a great nation]'" (Gen. 17:19–20).

   B. R. Yohanan in the name of R. Joshua b. Hananiah, "In this case the son of the servant-woman might learn from what was said concerning the son of the mistress of the household:

   C. "'Behold, I will bless him' refers to Isaac.

   D. "'...and make him fruitful' refers to Isaac.

   E. "'...and multiply him exceedingly' refers to Isaac.

   F. "'...As for Ishmael, I have informed you' through the angel." [The point is, Freedman (*Genesis,* Midrash Rabbah, vol. 1, p. 401, n. 4) explains: Ishmael could be sure that his blessing too would be fulfilled.]

   G. R. Abba b. Kahana in the name of R. Birai: "Here the son of the mistress of the household might learn from the son of the handmaiden:

   H. "'Behold, I will bless him' refers to Ishmael.

   I. "'...and make him fruitful' refers to Ishmael.

   J. "'...and multiply him exceedingly' refers to Ishmael.

   K. "And by an argument *a fortiori:* 'But I will establish my covenant with Isaac' (Gen. 17:21)."

2. A. Said R. Isaac, "It is written, 'All these are the twelve tribes of Israel' (Gen. 49:28). These were the descendants of the mistress [Sarah].

B. "But did Ishmael not establish twelve?

C. "The reference to those twelve is to princes, in line with the
    following verse: 'As princes and wind' (Prov. 25:14). [But the
    word for *prince* also stands for the word *vapor,* and hence the
    glory of the sons of Ishmael would be transient (Freedman,
    Genesis, Midrash Rabbah, vol. 1, p. 402, n. 2).]

D. "But as to these tribes [descended from Isaac], they are in
    line with this verse: 'Sworn are the tribes of the word, *se-
    lah'* (Hab. 3:9)." [Freedman (*Genesis,* Midrash Rabbah, vol. 1,
    p. 402, n. 3): The word for *tribe* and for *staff* or *rod,* in the
    cited verse, are synonyms, both meaning tribes, both mean-
    ing rods, and so these tribes would endure like rods that are
    planted.] (Gen. Rab. 47:5)

Numbers 1 and 2 take up the problem of the rather fulsome
blessing assigned to Ishmael. One authority reads the blessing
to refer to Isaac; the other maintains that the blessing refers indeed to Ishmael, and Isaac will gain that much more. Number 2
goes over the same issue, now with the insistence that the glory
of Ishmael will pass like vapor, while the tribes of Isaac will endure like well-planted rods. The polemic against Edom/Rome,
with its transient glory, is familiar. These brief passages suffice
to illustrate the main point, which concerns the theology of the
group as family and the working of that conception to encompass other families, the important ones placed into relationship
with Israel and so explained with reference to Israel.

The challenge of Christianity from the beginning had come
from its spiritualization of Israel. Here that challenge finds its
answer in the opposite and counterpart: the utter and complete
genealogization of Israel. To state matters negatively, the people
could no more conceive that they were not the daughters and
sons of their fathers and mothers than that they were not one
large family, that is, the family of Abraham, Isaac, and Jacob: Israel after the flesh. That is what "after the flesh" meant. The
powerful stress on the enduring merit of the patriarchs and
matriarchs, the social theory that treated Israel as one large,
extended family, the actual children of Abraham, Isaac, and Jacob — these now-familiar metaphors for the fleshly continuity
met head on the contrary position framed by Paul and restated
by Christian theologians from his time onward.

Israel as family therefore served a powerful polemical purpose in engaging with the new political facts of the age. But the theology did not originate in the fourth century. It originated in Scripture itself. Adopting the metaphor simply formed a stage in the metaphorization of Israel in the here and now by appeal to the Israel of Scripture. The potential of Israel as family existed as soon as thinkers about the social entity, Israel, realized that they and their contemporaries in the here and now constituted that same Israel that Scripture had portrayed. The family proved remarkably apt for the requirements of the new era, and that is why that definition of "Israel" fully came to realization in just this age. "Family" explained the composition of the household, an economic unit of production. "Family" accounted for the interrelationships of households of a certain sort — the Jewish sort — in a mixed village or in a village made up of only Jewish households. The metaphor of family allowed Jews to relate their own social entity to those other entities whose political presence they chose to acknowledge. In all, the power of the theology lay in its possibility of joining all social entities, whether groups, whether classes, whether of another order altogether, into a single and uniform entity: "the families of humanity," whether of Israel or of Esau. The metaphor of family (whether of Israel or Esau) thus left Israel as a separate "species" — as a different and separate family — but not alone among the genus "family." Sages found self-evident the fact that they — Israel — formed a group unlike other groups. They were not merely the better wing of a common family.

"Israel," then, stood for not only a different family among families but also a different people or nation among entities of the same genus. Long before the advent of Christianity, Jews — quite naturally thinking of themselves within the biblical record as embodying, in the present, the people Scripture had called "Israel" — had attained consciousness of their singularity among the peoples or nations of the world. In the debate with Christianity, sages evoked not only "family" but also "nation" or "people," an altogether political entity. In framing the theology of a social entity like, yet not alike, all other social entities — hence a nation, but a singular nation — sages prepared for their adversaries yet a second, if closely related, point-by-point reply to a critical challenge, in addition to the theology deriving from the family. The reason sages required this second definition of Israel — Israel as a nation unlike other nations — is that, for their part, the Christians spoke in political, not only genealogical, terms. In explaining the social entity constituted by them they too invoked the theology of people or nation — one of a peculiar order, to be sure. Consequently, the polemical task directed attention to the theology built not upon genealogy but upon a different sort of polity.

4

Israel and (Christian) Rome

The Christians from the beginning saw themselves as a people without a past, a no-people, a people gathered from the peoples. Who they claimed to be could hardly be derived from who they had been. Identifying with ancient Israel was a perfectly natural and correct initiative, well-founded on the basis of the Christian canon, encompassing the Hebrew Scriptures as "the Old Testament." It admirably accounted for the Christian presence in humanity, provided a past, explained to diverse people what they had in common. One problem from Christian theologians' perspective demanded solution: the existing Israel, the Jewish people, which revered the same Scriptures and claimed descent, after the flesh, from ancient Israel.

These — the Jews — traced their connection to ancient Israel, seeing the connection as both natural and supernatural. The family tie, through Abraham, Isaac, and Jacob, as we saw, formed a powerful apologetic indeed. The Jews furthermore pointed to their family record, the Scriptures, to explain whence they came and who they were. So long as the two parties to the debate shared the same subordinated political circumstance, Jewry could quite nicely hold its own in the debate. But with the shift in the politics of the empire, the terms of debate changed. The parvenu became paramount: the Christian party to the debate invoked its familiar position now with the power of the state in support.

The confrontation with Christianity in sages' thought took the form of a family dispute about who is the legitimate heir to the same ancestor. Judaic sages and Christian theologians addressed the same issue in pretty much the same terms, with a

71

single mode of argument, appealing to a shared body of facts —
the Scriptures — joining the two into a common debate. The
several threads of the dispute between Judaism and Christianity draw together into a tight fabric: the shift in the character
of politics, marked by the epochal triumph of Christianity in
the state, bears profound meaning for the messianic mission of
the Church and, further, imparts a final judgment on the salvific
claim of the competing nations of God — the Church and Israel.

What possible answer can sages have proposed to this in-
dictment? Since at the heart of the matter lies the Christians'
claim that scriptural Israel persists in the salvific heritage that
has passed to the Christians, sages reaffirm that scriptural Israel persists — just as Paul had framed matters, to which we
return in the concluding part of this chapter — after the flesh,
an unconditional and permanent status. But that consideration
formed only part of the matter. Another part concerned the political entity Israel, not merely the genealogical entity "children
of Abraham and Sarah." The issue addressed the holiness of Israel as political entity, people or nation. That accounts for the
joining of two metaphors, the one drawn from genealogy, the
other from politics.

A cogent and propositional commentary to the book of Leviticus, Leviticus Rabbah, ca. 400–450 C.E., reads the laws of
the ongoing sanctification in nature of the life of Israel as an
account of the rules of the onetime salvation in history of the
polity of Israel. To the framers of Leviticus Rabbah, one point
of emphasis proved critical: Israel remains "Israel," the Jewish
people, after the flesh, not only because Israel today contin-
ues the family begun by Abraham, Isaac, Jacob, Joseph, and
the other tribal founders and bears the heritage bequeathed by
them. Israel is what it is also because of its character as holy nation — not merely family. For salvific issues addressed not solely
to individuals but to concerns of history and eschatology frame
themselves as political, dealing with corporate social entities.

Maintaining, as the Christian theologians did, that Israel
would see no future salvation amounted to declaring that Israel, the Jewish people (no longer merely family), pursued no
worthwhile purpose in continuing to endure. Indeed, in light of
Paul's use of the theology of genealogy, the theology of the fam-

ily could not serve to convey the propositions that Israel (after the flesh) had had its salvation in the return to Zion and would have any future salvation at all. Accordingly, from the perspective of the Christian theologians, the shift from genealogical to political metaphors was necessary. When the argument joined the question Who is Israel? to the question Who enjoys salvation? the theology therefore shifted from family to political entity.

This brings us once more to Rome as a state — a nation, a people — *within the genus of Israel as a nation or a people*. In what is to follow, we see how Rome as family shades over into Rome as an empire and state, comparable to Israel as a nation or state — and as the coming empire too. That shading explains why we have called the treatment of Rome a special problem. For while "Rome" stands for "Esau," the comparison of Rome and Israel moves onto fresh ground, comparing Rome to animals as well as to the near family. We have already seen the adumbration of the position that, in Leviticus Rabbah, would come to remarkably rich expression. For Rome now stood for much more than merely a place among other places, or even a people or nation among peoples or nations. Rome took up a place in the unfolding of the empires — Babylonia, Media, Greece, then Rome. Israel takes its place in that unfolding pattern and hence is consubstantial with Babylonia, Media, Greece, and Rome. In that context, Rome and Israel do form counterparts and opposites.

Still more important, Rome is the penultimate empire on earth. Israel will constitute the ultimate one. That message, seeing the shifts in world history in a pattern and placing at the apex of the shift Israel itself, directly and precisely takes up the issue made urgent just now: the advent of the Christian emperors. Why do I maintain that in the characterization of Rome as the fourth and penultimate empire/animal, sages address issues of their own day? Because Rome, among the successive empires, bears special traits, most of which derive from the distinctively Christian character of Rome. It now becomes clear that we have moved very far from the genealogical theology.

Now Rome is like Israel in a way in which no other state or nation is like Israel, and, consequently, in the odd metaphors of Rome as an animal unlike other animals or Rome as an empire unlike other empires, we have to appeal to a special relationship between Rome and Israel. And that special relationship, already prepared, can only be genealogical. How so? Rome's relation to Israel — the ways in which it is both like and not like Israel — emerges as dissimilar to that of any other people or nation; and, it follows, Israel's relation to Rome — the ways in which it is like and unlike Rome — is dissimilar to its relation to any other people or nation.

The most suggestive disposition of Rome moved beyond the theory of the family. Esau is compared to a pig. The reason for the aptness of the analogy is simple. The pig exhibits public traits expected of a "suitable beast," in that it shows a cloven hoof, such as the laws of acceptable beasts require. But the pig does not exhibit the inner traits of a suitable beast, in that it does not chew the cud. Accordingly, the pig confuses and deceives. The polemic against Esau (= Rome) is simple. Rome claims to be Israel in that it adheres to the Old Testament, that is, the written Torah of Sinai. Specifically, Rome is represented as only Christian Rome can have been represented: it superficially *looks* kosher, but it is unkosher. Pagan Rome cannot ever have looked kosher, but Christian Rome, with its appeal to continuity with ancient Israel, could and did and moreover claimed to. It bore some traits that validate but lacked others that validate — just as Jerome said of Israel. It would be difficult to find a more direct confrontation between two parties to an argument. Now the issue is the same: Who is the true Israel? And the proof-texts are the same, and, moreover, the proof-texts are read in precisely the same way. Only the conclusions differ!

The polemic represented in the Talmud of the Land of Israel, Genesis Rabbah, and Leviticus Rabbah by the symbolization of Christian Rome makes a number of simple points. First, Christians are no different from, and no better than, pagans; they are essentially the same. Christians' claim to form part of Israel then requires no serious attention. Since Christians came to Jews with precisely that claim, the sages' response — they are another Babylonia — bears a powerful polemic charge. But that is not the whole story, as we see. Second, just as Israel had survived Babylonia, Media, and Greece, so would they endure to see the end of Rome (whether pagan, whether Christian).

But there is a third point; Rome really does differ from the earlier, pagan empires, and that polemic shifts the entire discourse, once we hear its symbolic vocabulary properly. For the new Rome really does differ from the old. Christianity is not merely part of a succession of undifferentiated modes of paganism. The symbols assigned to Rome attributed worse, more dangerous traits than those assigned to the earlier empires. The pig pretends to be clean, just as the Christians give the signs of adherence to the God of Abraham, Isaac, and Jacob. That much the passage concedes. But the pig is not clean: it exhibits only some, not all, of the required indications. And Rome is not Israel, even though it shares Israel's Scripture.

That brings us to that mixture of metaphors in which genealogy explains relationships between polities. Let us begin with a simple example of how ubiquitous is the shadow of Ishmael/Esau/Edom/Rome. Wherever in Genesis Rabbah sages reflect on future history, their minds turn to their own day. They found the hour difficult, because Rome, now Christian, claimed that very birthright and blessing that they understood to be theirs alone. Christian Rome posed a threat without precedent. Now another dominion, besides Israel's, claimed the rights and blessings that sustained Israel. Wherever in Scripture they turned, sages found comfort in the iteration that the birthright, the blessing, the Torah, and the hope — all belonged to them and to none other. Here we see a statement of that view, in the ample and handsomely articulated version of Leviticus Rabbah:

9.　A.　Moses foresaw what the evil kingdoms would do [to Israel].

　　B.　"The camel, rock badger, and hare" (Deut. 14:7). [Compare: "Nevertheless, among those that chew the cud or part the hoof, you shall not eat these: the camel, because it chews the cud but does not part the hoof, is unclean to you. The rock badger, because it chews the cud but does not part the hoof, is unclean to you. And the hare, because it chews the cud but does not part the hoof, is unclean to you. And the pig, because it parts the hoof and is cloven-footed, but does not chew the cud, is unclean to you" (Lev. 11:4–8).]

　　C.　The camel (*GML*) refers to Babylonia, [in line with the following verse of Scripture: "O daughter of Babylonia, you who are to be devastated!] Happy will be he who requites (*GML*) you, with what you have done to us" (Ps. 147:8).

D. "The rock badger" (Deut. 14:7) — this refers to Media.

E. Rabbis and R. Judah b. R. Simon.

F. Rabbis say, "Just as the rock badger exhibits traits of uncleanness and traits of cleanness, so the kingdom of Media produced both a righteous man and a wicked one."

G. Said R. Judah b. R. Simon, "The last Darius was Esther's son. He was clean on his mother's side and unclean on his father's side."

H. "The hare" (Deut 14:7) — this refers to Greece. The mother of King Ptolemy was named "Hare" [in Greek: *lagos*].

I. "The pig" (Deut. 14:7) — this refers to Edom [Rome].

J. Moses made mention of the first three in a single verse and the final one in a verse by itself [Deut. 14:7, 8]. Why so?

K. R. Yohanan and R. Simeon b. Laqish.

L. R. Yohanan said, "It is because [the pig] is equivalent to the other three."

M. And R. Simeon b. Laqish said, "It is because it outweighs them."

N. R. Yohanan objected to R. Simeon b. Laqish, " 'Prophesy, therefore, son of man, clap your hands [and let the sword come down twice, yea thrice]' (Ezra 21:14)."

O. And how does R. Simeon b. Laqish interpret the same passage? He notes that [the threefold sword] is doubled (Ezra 21:14). (Lev. Rab. 13:5)

In the apocalypticizing of the animals of Lev. 11:4–8/Deut. 14:7 (the camel, rock badger, hare, and pig), the pig, standing for Rome, again emerges as different from the others and more threatening than the rest. Just as the pig pretends to be a clean beast by showing the cloven hoof, but in fact is an unclean one, so Rome pretends to be just but in fact governs by thuggery. Edom does not pretend to praise God but only blasphemes. It does not exalt the righteous but kills them. These symbols concede nothing to Christian monotheism and veneration of the Torah of Moses (in its written medium). Of greatest importance, while all the other beasts bring further ones in their wake, the pig does not: "It does not bring another kingdom after it." It will restore the crown to the one who will truly deserve it, Israel. Esau will be judged by Zion (so Obad. 1:21). Now how has the symbolization delivered an implicit message? It is in the treatment of Rome as distinct from, but essentially equivalent to, the former kingdoms.

This seems to me a stunning way of saying that the now-Christian empire in no way requires differentiation from its pagan predecessors. The only change has been that matters have gotten worse. Beyond Rome, standing in a straight line with the others, lies the true shift in history, the rule of Israel and the cessation of the dominion of the (pagan) nations. Rome in the fourth century became Christian. Sages responded by facing that fact quite squarely and saying, "Indeed, it is as you say, a kind of Israel, an heir of Abraham as your texts explicitly claim. But we remain the sole legitimate Israel, the bearer of the birthright — we and not you. So you are our brother: Esau, Ishmael, Edom." And the rest follows.

The contrast between Israel and Esau produced the following anguished observation. But here the Rome alluded to is not yet Christian, so far as the clear reference is concerned. A further important point is that, for the text, Esau/Rome rules now, but Jacob/Israel will follow in due course. This claim is made explicit:

2. A. "And Jacob sent messengers before him":

   B. To this one [Esau] whose time to take hold of sovereignty would come before him [namely, before Jacob, since Esau would rule, then Jacob would govern].

   C. R. Joshua b. Levi said, "Jacob took off the purple robe and threw it before Esau, as if to say to him, 'Two flocks of starlings are not going to sleep on a single branch' [so we cannot rule at the same time].' "

3. A. " . . . to Esau his brother":

   B. Even though he was Esau, he was still his brother. (Gen. Rab. 75:4)

Numbers 2 and 3 make a stunning point: Esau remains Jacob's brother, and that Esau rules before Jacob will. The application to contemporary affairs cannot be missed, both in the recognition of the true character of Esau — a brother! — and in the interpretation of the future of history. This same point is made in another way in the following:

1. A. "These are the kings who reigned in the land of Edom be-
        fore any king reigned over the Israelites: Bela the son of Beor
        reigned in Edom, the name of his city being Dinhabah" (Gen.
        36:31–32):

    B. R. Isaac commenced discourse by citing this verse: "Of the
        oaks of Bashan they have made your oars" (Ezra 27:6).

    C. Said R. Isaac, "The nations of the world are to be compared
        to a ship. Just as a ship has its mast made in one place and its
        anchor somewhere else, so their kings: 'Samlah of Masrekah'
        (Gen. 36:36), 'Shaul of Rehobot by the river' (Gen. 36:27), and:
        'These are the kings who reigned in the land of Edom before
        any king reigned over the Israelites.' "

2. A. ["An estate may be gotten hastily at the beginning, but the
        end thereof shall not be blessed" (Prov. 20:21)]: "An estate
        may be gotten hastily at the beginning": "These are the kings
        who reigned in the land of Edom before any king reigned
        over the Israelites."

    B. "...but the end thereof shall not be blessed": "And saviors
        shall come up on mount Zion to judge the mount of Esau"
        (Obad. 1:21). (Gen. Rab. 83:1)

Number 1 contrasts the diverse origin of Roman rulers with the uniform origin of Israel's king in the house of David. No. 2 makes the same point still more forcefully. How so? H. Freedman makes sense of number 2 as follows: though Esau was the first to have kings, his land will eventually be overthrown.[1] So the point is that Israel will have kings after Esau no longer does, and the verse at hand is made to point to the end of Rome, a striking revision to express the importance in Israel's history of events in the lives of the patriarchs.

1. A. "These are the kings who reigned in the land of Edom be-
        fore any king reigned over the Israelites: Bela the son of Beor
        reigned in Edom, the name of his city being Dinhabah" (Gen.
        36:31–32):

---

1. *Genesis*, Midrash Rabbah, ed. H. Freedman and M. Simon (New York: Soncino, 1983), p. 766, n. 3.

B. Said R. Aibu, "Before a king arose in Israel, kings existed in Edom: 'These are the kings who reigned in the land of Edom before any king reigned over the Israelites.' " [Freedman (*Genesis,* Midrash Rabbah, p. 766, n. 4): "1 Kgs. 22:48 states, 'There was no king in Edom, a deputy was king.' This refers to the reign of Jehoshaphat. Subsequently in Jehoram's reign, Edom revolted and 'made a king over themselves' (2 Kgs. 8:20). Thus from Saul to Jehoshaphat, in which (time) Israel had eight kings, Edom had no king but was ruled by a governor of Judah. Aibu observes that this was to balance the present period, during which Edom had eight kings while Israel had none. For that reason, Aibu employs the word for deputy when he wishes to say 'existed' thus indicating a reference to the verse in the book of Kings quoted above."]

C. R. Yosé bar Haninah said, "[Alluding to a mnemonic, with the first Hebrew letter for the word for kings, judges, chiefs, and princes:] When the one party [Edom] was ruled by kings, the other party [Israel] was ruled by judges; when one side was ruled by chiefs, the other side was ruled by princes."

D. Said R. Joshua b. Levi, "This one set up eight kings and that one set up eight kings. This one set up Bela, Jobab, Husham, Samlah, Shaul, Hadad, Baalhanan, and Hadar. The other side set up Saul, Ishbosheth, David, Solomon, Rehoboam, Abijah, Asa, and Jehoshaphat.

E. "Then Nebuchadnezzar came and overturned both: 'That made the world as a wilderness and destroyed the cities thereof' (Isa. 14:17).

F. "Evil-merodach came and exalted Jehoiakin, Ahasuerus came and exalted Haman." (Gen. Rab. 83:2)

The passage once more stresses the correspondence between Israel's and Edom's governments, respectively. The reciprocal character of their histories is then stated in a powerful way, with the further implication that, when the one rules, the other waits. So now Israel waits, but it will rule. The same point is made in what follows, but the expectation proves acute and immediate.

3. A. "Magdiel and Iram: these are the chiefs of Edom, that is Esau, the father of Edom, according to their dwelling places in the land of their possession" (Gen. 36:42):

B. On the day on which Litrinus came to the throne, there appeared to R. Ammi in a dream this message: "Today Magdiel has come to the throne."

C. He said, "One more king is required for Edom [and then Israel's turn will come]."

4. A. Said R. Hanina of Sepphoris, "Why was he called Iram? For he is destined to amass [a word using the same letters] riches for the king-messiah."

B. Said R. Levi, "There was the case of a ruler in Rome who wasted the treasuries of his father. Elijah of blessed memory appeared to him in a dream. He said to him, 'Your fathers collected treasures and you waste them.'

C. "He did not budge until he filled the treasuries again." (Gen. Rab. 83:4)

Number 3 presents once more the theme that Rome's rule will extend only for a foreordained and limited time, at which point the Messiah will come. Number 4 explains the meaning of the name Iram. The concluding statement also alleges that Israel's saints even now make possible whatever wise decisions Rome's rulers make. That forms an appropriate conclusion to the matter. Ending in the everyday world of the here and now, sages attribute to Israel's influence anything good that happens to Israel's brother, counterpart, opposite, whether family, whether polity, Rome.

Representing Israel as singular invokes a narrowly political theology: nation or people, in the same genus as others, but, among them, singular and special by reason of service to God. But as soon as Rome enters discourse, that original theory fails, for reasons intrinsic to the conflicting claims. Rome too claims to serve God, the same God in the same way. The political theory fails, even while the political issues prevail. Accordingly, we find a reversion, when it comes to Rome in particular, to the genealogical theory, now framed in terms that, at their foundations, can be only political. So the family at one and the same time constitutes the people or nation. The upshot is the same.

But there is one important difference: now Israel is represented as unique. The sages set forth the view that the Israel that they saw every day formed a unique social entity. They concentrated their thought on the particularities of the Israel they saw every day, yielding a conception of Israel as sui generis, and, in seeing Israel as unique, they left off the matter of comparison, contrast, and classification. Seeing the social group as unlike all other social groups represents an act of comparison and contrast. This comparative view of Israel as sui generis — as sustained in the documents at hand as it was rare in the Mishnah — is revealed blatantly in two traits of the documents we have just been examining. First, we find a sustained interest in the natural laws governing Israel in particular, statements of the rules of the group's history viewed as a unique entity within time. Sentences out of the factual record of the past are formed into a cogent statement of the laws of Israel's destiny, laws unique to this social entity. Second, the teleology of those laws for an Israel that was sui generis focused upon salvation at the end of history, that is, an eschatological teleology formed for a social entity embarked on its own lonely journey through time.

Israel beyond all metaphor, unavailable for comparison and contrast, that people "dwelling alone," was now the object of intense study on the part of the thoughtful sages who governed from day to day but also gazed beyond the far horizon. Indeed, seeing Israel as sui generis and not merely an abstraction and instrumentality for classification of entities may well represent a perspective natural to a group within the political class of the population. For, one may suppose, concrete issues in the here and now tended to highlight differences between group and group and to obliterate those points in common that permitted comparison in the philosophical mode. Portraying themselves as engaged with a real social group on a day-to-day basis, sages searched within the life of that group for the rules and orderly regulations that governed it. Seeking commonalities of pattern within the group, they centered their interest on what they deemed particular to Israel.

Definitions of "Israel" are expressed not only in explicit terms but also in the implicit terms yielded by how people discuss the social entity. In Leviticus Rabbah the conception of Israel as sui generis reaches expression in an implicit statement that Israel is subject to its own laws, which are distinct from the laws governing all other social entities. These laws may be discerned in the factual, scriptural record of Israel's past, and that past, by definition, belongs to Israel alone. It follows, therefore, that by discerning the regularities in Israel's history, implicitly understood as unique to Israel, sages recorded the view that Israel, like God, is not subject to analogy or comparison. Accordingly, while not labeled a genus unto itself, Israel is treated in that way.

To understand how this view of Israel comes to expression, we have to trace the principal mode of thought characteristic of the authorship of Leviticus Rabbah. It is an exercise in proving hypotheses by tests of concrete facts. The hypotheses derive from the theology of Israel. The tests are worked out by reference to those given facts of social history that Scripture, for its part, contributes. The authorship at hand treated Scripture as a set of facts. These facts concerned history, not nature, but they served, much as did the facts of nature used by the Greek natural philosophers, to prove or disprove hypotheses. The hypotheses concerned the social rules to which Israel was subjected, and the upshot was that Israel was subject to its own rules, revealed by the historical facts of Scripture.

The single most common way in which sages made the implicit statement that Israel *is* sui generis was their "as-if" mode of seeing Israel's reality. Sages read Israel's history not as it seems — that is, not as it would appear when treated in accord with the same norms as the histories of other social entities — but as a series of mysteries. The facts are not what appearances suggest. The deeper truth is not revealed in those events that happen, in common, to Israel and to (other) nations over the face of the earth. What is really happening to Israel is wholly other, different from what seems to be happening and what is happening to ordinary groups. The fundamental proposition pertinent to Israel in Leviticus Rabbah is that things are not what they seem. Israel's reality does not correspond to the perceived facts of this world.

Now if we ask ourselves the source of this particular mode of thinking about Israel, we find no difficulty in identifying the point of origin. The beginning of seeing Israel as if it were other than the here-and-now social group people saw lay in the original theory of the social group. When people looked at themselves, their households and villages, their regions and language-group, and thought to themselves, "What more are we? What else are we?" they began that process of abstraction that took the form of an intellectual labor of comparison, contrast, and analogy. The group is compared to something else (or to nothing else) and hence is treated as not fully represented by the here and now but as also representative, itself, of something else beyond. And that very mode of seeing things, lying in the foundations of the Mishnah's authorship's thought, implicit in the identification of the survivors as the present avatar of Scripture's Israel, yielded an ongoing process of metaphorization.

The original use of the metaphor "Israel" to serve as the explanation of who the surviving groups were made it natural, from that time forward, to see Israel under the aspect of the "as-if." How this mode of thought worked itself out in the documents we have been examining is clear. The exegetes at hand maintained that a given statement of Scripture stood for and signified something other than that to which the verse openly referred. If — as was a given for these exegetes — water stands for Torah, then the skin disease mentioned in Leviticus 13 (in Hebrew called *saraat* and translated as leprosy) stands for, is caused by, evil speech. In this case, the reference to one thing means some other thing entirely. This mode of thought is simple.

And what is decisive for our inquiry is that *that mode of thought pertained to Israel alone.* Solely in the case of Israel did one thing symbolize another, speak not of itself but of some other thing entirely. When other social entities, for example, Babylonia, Persia, or Rome, stood for something else, it was in relationship to Israel. When these other entities are treated in a neutral context, by contrast, we find no metaphors: for example, Alexander of Macedonia in the story considered earlier is a person, and no symbol stands for that person. When Greece appears in the sequence of empires leading finally to the rule of Israel, then Greece may be symbolized by the hare. And there is another side of the matter too. Other things (the bear, the eagle) could stand for the empires, but — in that metaphorical context — then "Israel" stands only for itself. Whichever way

we have it, therefore, implicit in that view and mode of thought
is the notion of "Israel" as sui generis, lacking all counterpart
or parallel entities for purposes of comparison and contrast.
Transitive comparison and contrast is precisely the confirma-
tion of Israel as intransitive and sui generis. The importance
of the mode of reading Scripture "as if" it meant something
else than what it said, in the case of the exegesis of Leviticus
Rabbah, should not be missed. What lies beneath or beyond
the surface — there is the true reality, the world of truth and
meaning.

This mode of thinking about Israel applies a prevailing hermeneutic. A common object or symbol really represented an
uncommon one. Nothing says what it means. All statements
carry deeper meaning, which inheres in other statements altogether. Accordingly, the single prevalent literary construction
and message associated with this frame of mind are this: things
are never what they seem. All things demand interpretation. Interpretation begins in the search for analogy, for that to which
the thing is likened, hence the deep sense in which all exegesis
at hand is parabolic. It is a quest for that for which the thing
in its deepest structure stands. When sages represented Israel
as sui generis in the manner just now spelled out, they therefore brought to bear upon that social entity, the social group,
a mode of thought deriving to begin with from their manner
of reading Scripture. And, when we consider their ordering of
matters, we have further to observe that they read Scripture the
way Scripture taught them, to begin with, to encounter God:
"in our image, after our likeness," that is, metaphorically. Once
more we find ourselves following theological sociology into the
realm of theological anthropology.

Since the exegetes — by definition — applied the mode of
thought at hand solely to Israel, not to the nations, it follows
that Israel constituted an entity that was sui generis. For its affairs alone generated that search for a meaning different and
deeper than the one that floated at the surface. The Jews of
this period (and not then alone), so long used to calling themselves God's first love, were seeing others with greater worldly
influence and with reason to claim that same advantaged relationship to God. Not in mind only, but still more in the politics

of the world, the people that remembered its origins along with the very creation of the world and founding of humanity, that recalled how it alone served, and serves, the one and only God, for more than three hundred years had confronted a quite different existence. The radical disjuncture between the way things were and the way Scripture said things were supposed to be — and in actuality would some day become — surely imposed an unbearable tension. It was one thing for the slave born to slavery to endure. It was another for the free man sold into slavery to accept that same condition.

The vanquished people, the nation that had lost its city and its Temple, that had, moreover, produced another nation from its midst to take over its Scripture and much else, could not bear too much reality. That defeated people then found refuge in a mode of thought that trained vision to see things otherwise than as the eyes perceived them. Among the diverse ways by which the weak and subordinated accommodate to their circumstance, the one of iron-willed pretense is most likely to yield the mode of thought at hand: things never are, because they cannot be, what they seem.

What happens in the writings of Judaism, represented by Genesis Rabbah and Leviticus Rabbah, is that, reading one thing in terms of something else, the builders of the documents systematically adopted for Israel in their day the reality of Scripture, its history and doctrines — again with the consequence that Israel constituted a social entity that was sui generis, now once more by definition. They transformed that unique history from a sequence of onetime events, leading from one place to some other, into an ever-present mythic world. No longer was there one Moses, one David, one set of happenings of a distinctive and never-to-be-repeated character. Now whatever happens that the thinkers propose to take account of must enter and be absorbed into that established and ubiquitous pattern and structure founded in the patterns of Scripture's truth. It is not that biblical history repeats itself. Rather, biblical history no longer constitutes history as a story of things that happened once, long ago, and pointed to some one moment in the future. Rather, it becomes an account of things that happen every day — hence, an ever-present mythic world.

The upshot was that Israel now lived on a mythic plane of being, an eternity that happened to be caught up in time, so to speak, but truly, a social entity different in genus, not only in species.

What the sages now proposed was a reconstruction of Israel's social existence along the lines of the ancient design of Scripture as they read it. That meant that, from a sequence of onetime and linear events, everything that happened was turned into a repetition of known and already experienced paradigms — hence, once more, a mythic being of a unique social entity. The source and core of the myth, of course, derive from Scripture — Scripture reread, renewed, and reconstructed along with the society that revered Scripture. So, to summarize, the mode of thought that dictated the issues and the logic of the document, telling the thinkers to see one thing in terms of something else, addressed Scripture in particular and collectively. And thinking as they did, the framers of the documents saw Scripture in a new way, just as they saw their own circumstance afresh, rejecting their world in favor of Scripture's, reliving Scripture's world in their own terms.

The doctrinal substance of the theory of Israel as sui generis may be stated in a single paragraph, as follows, using as our source Leviticus Rabbah in particular.

God loves Israel and so gave them the Torah, which defines their life and governs their welfare (the position noted above, when God explains God's particular concern for Israel by reason of Israel's cleaving to God). Israel is alone in its category (sui generis), which is proved by the fact that what is a virtue to Israel is a vice to any other nation; what is life-giving to Israel is poison to the Gentiles. True, Israel sins, but God forgives that sin, having punished the nation on account of it. Such a process has yet to come to an end, but it will culminate in Israel's complete regeneration. Meanwhile, Israel's assurance of God's love lies in the many expressions of special concern for even the humblest and most ordinary aspects of the national life: the food the nation eats, the sexual practices by which it procreates. These life-sustaining, life-transmitting activities draw God's special interest, as a mark of his general love for Israel. Israel then is supposed to achieve its life in conformity with the marks of God's love. These indications moreover signify the character of Israel's difficulty, namely, subordination to the nations in general, but to the fourth kingdom, Rome, in particular. Both food laws and skin diseases stand for the nations. There is yet another category of sin, also collective and generative of collective punishment, and that is social. The moral character of Israel's life, the treatment of people by one another, the practice of gossip and small-scale thuggery — these too draw down divine penalty. The nation's fate therefore corresponds to its moral condition. The moral condition, however, emerges not only from the current generation. Israel's richest hope lies in the merit of the ancestors, thus in the scriptural record of the merits attained by the founders of the nation, those who originally brought it into being and gave it life.

If we now ask about further recurring themes or topics, there is one that is utterly commonplace. It is expressed by recurrent lists of events in Israel's (unique) history, meaning, in this context, Israel's history solely in scriptural times, down through the return to Zion. The lists again and again ring the changes on the onetime events associated with the generation of the flood; Sodom and Gomorrah; the patriarchs and the sojourn in Egypt; the exodus; the revelation of the Torah at Sinai; the golden calf; the Davidic monarchy and the building of the Temple; Sennacherib, Hezekiah, and the destruction of northern Israel; Nebuchadnezzar and the destruction of the Temple in 586; the life of Israel in Babylonian captivity; Daniel and his associates; Mordecai and Haman. These events turn out to serve as paradigms of the everyday social reality of the community of Israel, perceived in the here and now: an "as-if" way of speaking about the social facts of sin and atonement, steadfastness and divine intervention, and equivalent lessons. We find, in fact, a fairly standard repertoire of scriptural heroes or villains, on the one side, and conventional lists of Israel's enemies and their actions and downfall, on the other. The boastful, for instance, include the generation of the flood, Sodom and Gomorrah, Pharaoh, Sisera, Sennacherib, Nebuchadnezzar, and the wicked empire (Rome) — contrasted to Israel, "despised and humble in this world." The four kingdoms recur again and again, always ending, of course, with Rome, with the repeated message that after Rome will come Israel. But Israel has to make this happen through its faith and submission to God's will. Lists of enemies ring the changes on Cain, the Sodomites, Pharaoh, Sennacherib, Nebuchadnezzar, Haman.

The catalogues of exemplary heroes and historical events provide a model of how contemporary events are to be absorbed into the biblical paradigm unique to Israel. Because biblical events exemplify recurrent happenings, sin and redemption, forgiveness and atonement, they lose their onetime character. At the same time and in the same way, current events find a place within the ancient, but eternally present, paradigmatic scheme. So no new historical events, other than exemplary episodes in the lives of heroes, demand narration because, through what is said about the past, what is happening in the times of the framers of Leviticus Rabbah also comes under consideration. This mode of dealing with biblical history and contemporary events produces two reciprocal effects. The first is the mythicization of biblical stories, their removal from the framework of ongoing, unique patterns of history and sequences of events and their transformation into accounts of things that happen all the time. The second is that contemporary events too lose all of their specificity and enter the paradigmatic framework of established mythic existence. So the Scripture's myth happens every day, and every day produces reenactments of the Scripture's myth. In concrete terms, this would seem to mean that nothing can be said about the unique social entity: if we speak of an entity unlike all others, then, by rights, we should not be able to make intelligible statements. But, as we see, sages can and do.

The basic mode of thought — denial of what is at hand in favor of a deeper reality — proves remarkably apt. The substance of thought concerning the unique social entity, beyond all theory, confronts the acute crisis of the present circumstance: Are we lost for good to the fourth empire, now-Christian Rome? No, says this mode of thought, we may yet be saved. Has God rejected us forever? No, aided by the merit of the patriarchs and matriarchs and of the Torah and religious duties, we gain God's love. What must we do to be saved? We must *do* nothing, we must *be* something: sanctified. That status we gain through keeping the rules that make Israel holy. So salvation is through sanctification, all embodied in Leviticus read as rules for the holy people.

The Messiah will come not because of what a pagan emperor does, nor, indeed, because of Jewish action either, but because of Israel's own moral condition. When Israel enters the right relationship with God, then God will respond to Israel's condition by restoring things to their proper balance. Israel cannot, but need not, so act as to force the coming of the Messiah. Israel can, however, attain the condition of sanctification, by forming a moral and holy community, to such a degree that God's response will follow the established prophecy of Moses and the prophets. So the basic doctrine of Leviticus Rabbah is the metamorphosis of Leviticus. Instead of holy caste, we deal with holy people. Instead of holy place, we deal with holy community, in its holy Land. The deepest exchange between reality and inner vision, therefore, comes at the very surface: the rereading of Leviticus in terms of a different set of realities from those to which the book, on the surface, relates. No other biblical book would have served so well; it had to be Leviticus. Only through what the framers did on that particular book could they deliver their astonishing message and vision.

Israel thus emerges as a unique social entity. What we have is the result of the mode of thought not of prophets or historians, but of philosophers and scientists: theologians. The framers propose not to lay down, but to discover, rules governing Israel's life. As we find the rules of nature by identifying and classifying facts of natural life, so we find rules of society by identifying and classifying the facts of social life. In both modes of inquiry we make sense of things by bringing together like specimens and finding out whether they form a species, then bringing together like species and finding out whether they form a genus — in all, classifying data and identifying the rules that make possible the classification. That sort of thinking lies at the deepest level of certain types of list making, those that involve offering a proposition and facts (for social rules) as much as a genus and its species (for rules of nature). Once discovered, the social rules of Israel's national life of course yield explicit syllogistic statements such as the following: God hates the arrogant and loves the humble; X is arrogant, and Y is humble; therefore, God hates X and loves Y.

The logical status of these syllogistic statements (based on facts and yielding propositions of their own), to which reasonable persons must accede, in context, is as secure and unassailable as the logical status of statements about physics, ethics, or politics, as these emerge in philosophical thought. What differentiates the statements is not their logical status — as sound, scientific philosophy — but only their subject matter, on the one side, and distinctive rhetoric, on the other. The heart of the matter lies in laying forth the rules of life — of Israel's life and salvation. These rules — particular to their subject, which is therefore sui generis — derive from the facts of history, as much as the rules of the Mishnah derive from the facts of society (and, in context, the rules of philosophy derive from the facts of nature). In their search for the rules of Israel's life and salvation, sages found their answer not in the onetime events of history but in paradigmatic facts, social laws of salvation of the unique social entity.

Part Two

The Church:
The Body of Christ

BRUCE CHILTON

5

Jesus and the Absence of Israel

While the Mishnah and Talmud are concerned to delineate Israel as a unique social entity, the teaching of Jesus simply fails to provide any definition of Israel. There are, to be sure, references to the word "Israel," in individual sayings with a meaning we will consider shortly (see Matt. 8:10; 10:6, 23; 15:24; 19:28; Mark 12:29; Luke 4:25, 27; 7:9; 22:30), but in every single case it is presupposed that the definition of Israel has already been settled. It is a point of reference that Jesus assumes he holds in common with his audience.

Jesus' own understanding of Israel can therefore be elicited only indirectly from our sources; there is no reasonable prospect of discovering a formal definition. That situation alerts us to a feature of Jesus' teaching that has not been sufficiently appreciated. He gives remarkably little attention to basic issues of social definition. He addresses an Israel he does not define, although in Galilee there was a substantial non-Jewish population.[1] He sends out his disciples to preach and act in his name and to shake off from them the very dust of any place that refuses to listen, all without explaining to them what their status is in relation to Israel (see Matt. 10:1–16; Mark 6:7–12; Luke 9:1–6). And, of course, he was executed by the Romans with the willing collaboration of Caiaphas, the most successful high priest of the first century. His execution was the result of his dispute concerning the correct conduct of worship in the Temple, but he

---

1. See Seán Freyne, "The Geography, Politics, and Economics of Galilee and the Quest for the Historical Jesus," in *Studying the Historical Jesus: Evaluations of the State of Current Research,* ed. Bruce D. Chilton and C. A. Evans, New Testament Tools and Studies 19 (Leiden: Brill, 1994), 75–121.

provided no formal guidance as to what precisely that worship should be.[2]

All of the vital aspects of his ministry — his public activity in preaching and healing, his commissioning of disciples to act as his representatives, his shameful death at the hands of the current Roman prefect — imply that Jesus contested the social definition of Israel. His activity in Galilee particularly (rather than Judaea) contests who Israel is, because the ambient environment there had been deeply influenced by Hellenism. His sending of apostles contests where Israel is to be found, because they are directed to some places and not others. His challenge of the cultic authorities in Jerusalem and their Roman backers contests why Israel should exist, because by the first century sacrifice in the Temple was widely agreed to be the single most important public activity of the people of God.

But all of this contestation is implicit, because Jesus assumes (as we have seen) that "Israel" is an agreed term of reference. Paradox is frequently a feature of Jesus' teaching, which is one reason his parables are as rich and satisfying as they are. But the issue of Israel does not seem to be a deliberate paradox. Jesus' concerns do not appear to have been consciously social, at least not at the level of abstract or practical organization.

John Calvin, the great reformer of the sixteenth century, undertook the task of providing his Geneva with a Christian constitution, in the conscious acknowledgment that Jesus had provided no blueprint for the creation of such an entity. Asked to return after a period of enjoyable exile in Strasbourg, he compared the task to the cross and remarked, "It would be far better to perish once for all than to be tormented again in that torture chamber."[3] He was aware of what Alfred Loisy, the Catholic Modernist, would put more cynically (if no less flamboyantly) at the end of the last century: Jesus announced the

---

2. See Bruce Chilton, *The Temple of Jesus: His Sacrificial Program within a Cultural History of Sacrifice* (University Park: Pennsylvania State University Press, 1992), 91–111, and idem, "Caiaphas," in *The Anchor Bible Dictionary*, ed. D. N. Freedman (New York: Doubleday, 1992), 1:803–6.

3. See his correspondence with Pierre Viret and the similar comment to Guillaume Farel; see T. H. L. Parker, *Portrait of Calvin* (Philadelphia: Westminster, 1961), 64.

coming of the kingdom of God, and what arrived instead was the Church.[4]

What Calvin and Loisy realized in their different ways is that Jesus provided the incentive for social revolution, for a distinctive definition of Israel, without actually defining that Israel itself. As a result, his followers acted in accord with differing and sometimes contradictory definitions, each framed within its own conditions and for its own constituency. The next chapter will discuss those earliest theologies of Israel. The present concern is with Jesus himself: What was his focus, such that he provided the incentive to revolutionize Israel without offering a definition of Israel? In order to address that question, I will analyze his own activity in Galilee, his policy of sending out apostles, and his conflict with the cultic authorities in Jerusalem.

Jesus' Activity in Galilee

In the previous volume of this series, I characterized the nature of Jesus' activity in Galilee.[5] His typical concern was to preach the kingdom of God and to heal in its name, usually by casting out unclean spirits. The kingdom in his theology was God's own activity. Because he saw it as what God himself was doing, the kingdom in Jesus' teaching is presented as the fulfillment of what can be known of the divine presence. This presentation occurs along five coordinates.

The kingdom is final in time, the goal and purpose of human endeavor (and in that sense eschatological). The kingdom is also transcendent, yearning to fill all things and therefore driving out what is contrary to it beforehand. The kingdom consists of love and therefore involves an ethical imperative. The kingdom,

---

4. The published form of the statement is in *L'Évangile et l'Église* (Paris: Picard, 1902), 255; its formulation has been dated around 1892. See Jean Carmignac, *Le Mirage de l'Eschatologie* (Paris: Letouzey et Ané, 1979), 151–55.

5. Details and discussion to support the summary that follows will be found there: see Jacob Neusner and Bruce D. Chilton, *Revelation: the Torah and the Bible,* Christianity and Judaism — The Formative Categories (Valley Forge: Trinity Press International, 1995), esp. chap. 5.

as God's, is holy and demands its own purity. Finally, the kingdom is asserting itself as divine power, which radiates outward to include those who respond to its pure love.[6]

Centering as it did on his awareness of divine activity, rather than simply on a given message about God, Jesus' own ministry is better understood as programmatic activity than merely as teaching. What he did was obviously inclusive of speech, especially parabolic speech, but his speech of the kingdom was self-consciously illustrative. He spoke of what the kingdom was *like*, of what God was doing, of how we might conceive of the kingdom, not of how exactly the kingdom could be categorized. His actions themselves, as he traveled and healed for the kingdom, are presented as parabolic: Jesus' casting out demons means the kingdom has come (so Matt. 12:28 ‖ Luke 11:20), and moving from place to place was part of the purpose for which God sent him (so Mark 1:38 ‖ Luke 4:43). Enacted parable and spoken parable are both attestations of the kingdom of God, within Jesus' estimate of his own activity.

Three stories are particularly striking in reference to the contested understanding of Israel within Jesus' programmatic activity. Jesus is said in the first to cast out and destroy a "legion" of demons on gentile territory (Matt. 8:28–34 ‖ Mark 5:1–20 ‖ Luke 8:26–39). The second finds him healing a centurion's servant (Matt. 8:5–13 ‖ Luke 7:1–10). The last portrays his encounter with a gentile woman who talks Jesus into healing her daughter (Matt. 15:21–28 ‖ Mark 7:24–30).

Each of the stories stems from a distinct source of the Gospels. Jesus' meeting with the legion was recounted within the cycle of James, Jesus' brother, while the source of Jesus' teaching known as "Q" provides the story of the centurion, and the circle of Peter transmitted the encounter with the gentile woman. The particular characteristics and theologies of those different communities and their traditions will concern us in the next chapter.[7]

---

6. A full treatment of these dimensions of the kingdom as conveying the nature of Jesus' preaching is available in Bruce Chilton, *Pure Kingdom: Jesus' Vision of God,* Studying the Historical Jesus 1 (Grand Rapids: Eerdmans, 1996).

7. In any case, the cycles were introduced and identified in Neusner and Chilton, *Revelation.*

Their consensus is what attracts our attention at the moment: *Jesus' activity of exorcising and healing must have contested the usual understanding of Israel in order to have produced three stories of this kind that were preserved within different cycles of tradition.* That will become all the more striking in the light of the next chapter, which will show that the distinct cycles developed distinct definitions of Israel.

Obviously, the characteristic theologies of the cycles have influenced the presentation of each story, and it is crucial to avoid the anachronism of reading a later understanding of the Church as Israel into the teaching of Jesus. After all, no circle of primitive Christianity claimed that Jesus himself said that he came to replace Israel. It is, in fact, a sign of the primitive origin of these stories that they involve a contested Israel, not a replaced Israel. Given that the sources in question emerged at an early stage in the development of the movement (the Petrine cycle and Q, ca. 35 C.E., the Jacobean cycle, ca. 40 C.E.), it is clear that the stories must have appeared earlier still, a fact that underlines their importance for the study of Jesus. Their very failure to spell out just what Israel is or should be signals their pedigree in the period before clear definition became the order of the day.

Each story proceeds by attributing a successful exorcism or healing to Jesus. Jesus himself saw exorcisms as attesting his message of the kingdom (see Matt. 12:28 ‖ Luke 11:20), and his reputation as a healer is attested in every major cycle of the Gospels. Unless he was clearly understood by his contemporaries to have exorcised and healed, it is all but impossible to explain why the sources say what they do.[8] What someone living today would have made of the events and the stories can not be known; what is historically evident is that those who lived at that time took them for actual exorcisms and/or healings. That gap between ancient and modern understanding is of interest, but it will not divert us here from considering how these primitive stories contest the understanding of Israel.

---

8. For a fuller discussion of the point, see Bruce D. Chilton, *Galilean Rabbi and His Bible* (Wilmington, Del.: Glazier, 1984), 71–78.

The Legion of Demons

We begin with what has traditionally been considered the most difficult of the three stories (here paraphrased, with no attempt to trace the details and causes of differences among the Synoptics). Jesus is placed on the eastern side of the Sea of Galilee, in explicitly gentile territory. The already emphatic impurity of the locale is, at it were, squared by the approach of a maniac who inhabits the *cemetery* of the Gerasenes. The unclean spirit within him calls himself "legion," an evident reference to the recent occupation by the Romans (under Pompey) and the use of the region of the Decapolis for administrative purposes.[9] Now we understand how impure the place is and why it is appropriate to think of it in terms of death itself. Finally, however, impurity squared becomes impurity cubed with the request of the demons to enter a herd of about two thousand pigs. The narrative puts Jesus in confrontation with uncleanness, if not to the nth degree, then cubed.

Jesus' characteristic activity within Galilee put him into contact with those whom many teachers would have considered of doubtful purity. The failure to pay tithe, for example, was held by Pharisees to render one unfit for fellowship (in the Mishnah, see the tractate Demai). A well-known saying of Jesus, widely held to be authentic, attests Jesus' own awareness that his habit of table-fellowship with dubious examples of Israel was notorious (see Matt. 11:19 ‖ Luke 7:34, from Q). But the story of the Gerasene maniac pushes the issue of uncleanness well beyond debatable questions: here is a man who lives in a cemetery in gentile territory occupied by the Romans, whose unclean spirit calls itself "legion" (troops) and likes the company of swine.

The maniac may or may not be understood to be an Israelite. His proximity to the pigs is no disqualification; Jesus' own parable of the wayward son conceives of pig keeping as the supreme symbol that a Jew has hit rock bottom (see Luke 15:11–32). The reference to Jesus as "the son of God Most High," however, probably suggests that the maniac is a Gentile, since "God Most High" is a title of the God of Israel that is classically used by

---

9. See John J. Rousseau and Rami Arav, *Jesus and His World: An Archaeological and Cultural Dictionary* (Minneapolis: Fortress, 1995), 85–87, 97–99.

non-Israelites (see Melchizedek in Gen. 14:19; Balaam in Num. 24:16; and the Philippian slave girl in Acts 16:17).

Whether the maniac is identified as a Jew or not, the outcome of his encounter is plainly indicated. The pigs are drowned, the demons are confined to the deep, and Jesus is cordially invited to depart from the area. His purity is such that he can indeed encounter what is triply impure, the gentile domain of Roman mortuary demons and swine, and the result is a disaster for uncleanness itself. Jesus can abide what is impure, but what is impure cannot survive before him.

Within its own particular terms of reference, the story of the legion of demons might be compared to the story of Nadab and Abihu, the sons of Aaron, in the Hebrew Bible (Lev. 10:1–3). When they offered an unauthorized, unwanted form of sacrifice by fire, they were themselves consumed with fire. As fire is the answer to fire in Leviticus, drowned pigs are the answer to impure spirits in the Synoptic Gospels. In both cases, the underlying dynamic of the narratives is that the pure and the impure are incompatible and that it is the pure that destroys the impure when they meet, by driving uncleanness to self-immolation.

The narrative of the demonic legion and the Gerasene swine is an explicit marker of the limits of Jesus' characteristic activity. Seán Freyne[10] has observed that Jesus is not placed by the Gospels in any of the urban centers that modern archaeologists have excavated. We can say much more about Sepphoris and Tiberias, for example, than was once the case, but we find Jesus there no more than in Tyre or Sidon. Fishing towns such as Bethsaida and Capernaum, agricultural settlements such as Nazareth and Chorazin, rather provided his focus of activity. Even in Jerusalem, we find him staying out in the village of Bethany. The story of the legion permits us to say why Jesus avoided the centers of Roman civilization in his area.

The very conception of the story projects Jesus' practice of purity as inclusive, willing to engage the man from the tombs, the request of the legion to enter the swine. But his apparent willingness to accede to their desire is a disaster for them and for the economy of the region. Implicitly, insofar as the demons

---

10. See Freyne, "Geography," 84, 120–21.

take the name of "legion," Roman hegemony itself is threatened. From the perspective of the story, Jesus did not avoid
Caesarea and Sepphoris and Tyre and Sidon because he feared
the contact of impurity; rather, his avoidance was a matter of
containing the power of his own purity. The whole irony of
the encounter is that Jesus' trip east, in the direction of Roman
influence, banishes the demons, kills the pigs, and upsets the
prosperity that the Romans and their legions have brought.

As purity delineated the Israel that the Pharisees attained
to and that the Essenes insisted upon, so purity was at the
center of Jesus' program. According to his ideal, the purity of
the kingdom could be celebrated in meals of fellowship within
Israel. The generic purity of Israel was assumed, without the
addition of pharisaic or Essene rules of tithing and preparation.
But within Jesus' practice, precisely which Israel was assumed
to be pure? Jesus' own activity draws us a map of Israel as
communities in which Jewish settlements, supported by fishing
and/or agriculture, supported themselves and were productive
for other Jews. Those communities might be in the territory of
Herod Antipas (Nazareth, Capernaum, and Chorazin are examples) or in the territory of Herod Philip (Bethsaida being an
example). Political boundaries as such do not seem to have been
considered an issue.

What was at issue, the story of the legion informs us, was
the intent to join the circle of Israel by means of the practice
of purity. Absent that intent, contact with Jesus' purity might
be disastrous. Once purity in Jesus' teaching and practice is
understood to be a positive value, the condition of Israel that
is consistent with the kingdom of God,[11] then the story of the
legion becomes sensible. Apart from the context of purity, the
story seems to tell of an arbitrary display of power; within that
context, the story articulates the implicit limitation of Jesus'
ministry to nonurban Israel.

Within nonurban Israel, fellowship might be joined by the
offering of one's own produce, on the assumption that the prod-
ucts of Israel were suitably pure. At the same time, forgiveness
is clearly a feature of Jesus' movement, in which a regular

---

11. See Chilton, *Temple of Jesus*, 121–36.

prayer to be forgiven was characteristic (see Matt. 6:12 ‖ Luke 11:4). But to that which is outside Jesus' Israel, to the world of unclean spirits, of swine and cemeteries, of all that the legion represent, Jesus' purity is a threatening practice. There, generic cleanness may not be assumed, and forgiveness is neither asked nor offered; it is a world that is simply incompatible with Jesus' vision. The end of the story, in the request that Jesus depart, is the limiting boundary of what constitutes Israel.[12] As in the Mishnah, so for Jesus, Israel is marked off from non-Israel by the practice of purity. In Jesus' case, the purity at issue is more generic than in the Mishnah, a matter of producing more than tithing, and yet the fundamental, defining role of purity remains constant.

The Centurion's Servant

Purity is also a pivot on which the story of the healing of the centurion's servant turns (Luke 7:1–10 ‖ Matt. 8:5–13). Recent commentators, following the line of Rudolf Bultmann, have concentrated on the figure of Jesus and his ability to heal.[13] In fact, that aspect is better brought out by the related story of the healing of the royal official's son in the Gospel according to John (4:46–53).[14] The issue in the two versions of Q, Luke's and Matthew's,[15] is rather the contact — or the lack of contact — between Jesus and the centurion. Luke is generally considered to represent the recension of Q more directly than Matthew does, and in the present case it also better elucidates the issue of contact. For those reasons, Luke 7:1–10 will constitute the basis of my discussion.

The centurion is resident in Capernaum and is presumably

---

12. The concluding vignette, of the attempt of the maniac to follow Jesus (see Mark 5:18–20), is the product of the cycle of tradition in which the story was preserved; it will be discussed in the next chapter, pp. 120–125.

13. See Darrell L. Bock, *Luke,* Baker Exegetical Commentary on the New Testament (Grand Rapids: Baker, 1994), 639–45.

14. For the relationship between that story and a healing attributed to Ḥanina ben Dosa, see Chilton, *Galilean Rabbi,* 31–32.

15. The cataloguing of the differences between the two is not the concern here, but it does seem obvious that one version does not simply derive from the other, and that they both do not rely on exactly the same original.

attached to the military bureaucracy of Herod Antipas.[16] Although a Jew or proselyte might conceivably have served in such a position, the story hinges on the centurion's identity as a non-Jew. He does not approach Jesus himself; rather, a delegation of Jewish elders pleads his case, on the grounds that he "loves our people and himself built a synagogue for us." During this period, synagogues in Galilee were indistinguishable from private dwellings and were sometimes incorporated within them.[17] The benefaction of the centurion is therefore quite plausible.

The status of the centurion may be compared to that of Cornelius, the centurion whom Peter visits in Caesarea (Acts 10). He is described as pious and "fearing God," a righteous person with his household, faithful to the covenant with Israel in all but circumcision (see especially Acts 10:2, 4, 22, 31, 35). The practice of circumcision was loathsome to Graeco-Roman sensibilities, and to some people it was at odds with the philosophical appeal of Judaic monotheism. A group that saw the biblical institution as of purely symbolic significance is discussed by Philo of Alexandria, who opposed the group in *On the Migration of Abraham* 89–93. That the group was refuted by Philo reveals that it had made some headway in Alexandria. However, its position — attempting to make circumcision into something other than a cutting away of the foreskin — made no apparent progress in Galilee. The demarcation between a God-fearer and an Israelite was plain in Jesus' environment.

The position of the centurion in Capernaum therefore seems well defined, and his considerate approach to Jesus corresponds to his position. He assumes that he is not worthy for the famous rabbi to enter his house and that he should not even approach Jesus personally. The tradition of commentaries has so focused on the humility of the centurion that the obvious basis of his assumption has been ignored: *the centurion must have understood that Jesus limited his activity to Israel, as usually demar-*

---

16. See Bock, *Luke,* 635–36.
17. See Yoram Tasfrir, "On the Source of the Architectural Design of the Ancient Synagogues in the Galilee: A New Appraisal," in *Ancient Synagogues: Historical Analysis and Archaeological Discovery,* ed. D. Urman and P. V. M. Flesher, Studia Postbiblica 47 (Brill: Leiden, 1995), 70–86.

cated by circumcision. The story proceeds on the supposition that the spoken word will be the only contact between Jesus and the centurion, and the faith of the centurion is commended on that basis. It is his suggestion that Jesus' word of command will be as effective as his own order within his bureaucracy, and that is the course that the story follows.[18]

The narrative provides every opportunity for Jesus to insist that the boundary of the circumcised and the uncircumcised may be transgressed. That is just what occurs in the house of Cornelius in Acts 10, when Peter visits the Roman centurion in a way unlike Jesus' indirect encounter with the centurion in Capernaum. The difference between the two stories is a clear indication of the distinct change in the social constitution of Jesus' movement after the resurrection. From the point of view of understanding Jesus' own conception of Israel, the healing of the centurion's servant provides a plain paradigm.

The model of Israel as the circumference of Jesus' activity is so obvious, we can rightly ask: How is it that it has been missed by traditional commentators? The answer to that question is found in the context in which the saying that closes the story is read. "Not even in Israel have I found such faith!" That exclamation from Jesus, read within the cultural environment of Graeco-Roman Christianity, is naturally understood as a commendation of a believing God-fearer in preference to circumcised Israel. The immediate inference from the story would be that believing centurions and the like should be embraced by baptism and fellowship within the Church, as in the case of Cornelius in Acts. But that contrasting portrait of the centurion, distinct from a Jewish constituency and embraced in fellowship, is simply anachronistic within the context of the Galilean phase of Jesus' movement. At that phase, the narrative carefully draws the line between Israel and God-fearer and portrays Jesus as observing that line.

---

18. It is remarkable that the same hegemony that provides the negative image of the legion (of demons) also provides the positive image of the (centurion's) hierarchy. Evidently, Roman social structure as such was neither rejected nor embraced among those who told these stories. The issue was larger for them: How could the available structures of society be seen to resist or to welcome the kingdom of God?

Part of what is commended in the attitude of the centurion from Capernaum is his awareness of the limitation of feasible contact between himself and Jesus. Jesus' own direct activity is portrayed as concentrated on circumcised Israel and as available outside that circle only by indirection. It is emphatically the case that the centurion benefits from what Jesus does and says within Israel, but equally plain that his inclusion is always at one remove from Jesus. The definition of Israel that establishes this pattern is not spelled out here, and that is a concern to which we must be alert as we proceed.

The Syrophoenician Woman

The implicit Israel that Jesus addressed, whose formal definition is absent from the sources, consists of communities with certain clear characteristics. They live dependent upon the land or the sea, accept circumcision in their practice of the Torah, keep to their understandings of purity, and are in productive relationship with other communities of circumcised Israel. It is customary to envision Jesus as limiting his ministry to Galilee, but we have already found him on both sides of the Sea of Galilee (in the story of the "legion" [Matt. 8:28–34 ‖ Mark 5:1–20 ‖ Luke 8:26–39]), and his activity in or near Bethsaida presents him as crossing a political boundary (as we have observed; see Mark 6:45–52 and 8:22–26, for example).

Jesus' apolitical Israel could be found in odd places. Peter's famous confession of Jesus as Messiah is located in the vicinity of Ceasarea Philippi in both Matthew (16:13–20) and Mark (8:27–30).[19] Jesus' actual approach to the city itself, built by Herod Philip around the site of temples to the god Pan and to the emperor,[20] need have been no closer than Nazareth was to Sepphoris in the territory of Herod Antipas. There is no reason to believe that, having established the practice of avoiding cities in Galilee, he broke that habit as soon as he crossed a political boundary. Nonetheless, activity in the region of Cae-

---

19. The passage is interpreted in some detail in Neusner and Chilton, *Revelation,* chap. 6.
20. See Rousseau and Arav, *Jesus and His World,* 33–35.

sarea Philippi would scarcely be emblematic of a passionate nationalism or an exclusive understanding of purity.

The same might be said of Jesus' activity in the vicinity of Tyre and of Sidon,[21] which is where Jesus' encounter with a non-Jewish woman is sited in both Matthew (15:21–28) and Mark (7:24–30). The naming of both cities is not incidental, since the two are paired in a saying of Jesus that associates the two as examples of what God will one day judge (see Matt. 11:21–22 ‖ Luke 10:13–14). The fact that she is a woman and not Jewish marks her as impure: she does not engage in the regular practice of cleansing that menstruation and childbirth demand (see Leviticus 12, by way of example). The issue of impurity is underlined, in that she approaches Jesus on behalf of her daughter, seeking her release from what Mark calls an unclean spirit.

What rivets the attention in the story is the verbal victory of the woman, at the expense of Jesus.[22] He rebuffs her with the brutal parable that it is not good to take the bread that belongs to children and give it to dogs. She replies that even dogs are permitted to eat the scraps that have fallen under the table, and Jesus then announces the healing of the woman's daughter. The contrast with the story of the centurion in Capernaum is striking. The woman's location, her designation as a non-Jew with no evident interest in Judaism,[23] as well her sex and that of her daughter all represent her as impure in ways the centurion was not. Finally, she insists on the sort of direct encounter with Jesus that the centurion scrupulously avoided. Here, then, is a paradigmatic story of how Jesus dealt with evident impurity.

The sense of the paradigm is direct: Jesus accedes to the healing but avoids contact. Insofar as it implies a definition of Israel, the story of the Syrophoenician departs from the sense of the healing of the centurion's servant in attitude but not in substance. Where the centurion draws the line of purity between himself and Jesus in terms of his own unworthiness for fellow-

---

21. Ibid., 326–28.

22. See Joanna Dewey, "The Gospel of Mark," in *Searching the Scriptures,* vol. 2, *A Feminist Commentary,* ed. Elizabeth Schüssler Fiorenza (New York: Crossroad, 1994), esp. 470–509, 484–85.

23. She is described as a Canaanite in Matthew and as a Greek from Syrophoenicia in Mark.

ship with the rabbi, the Syrophoenician woman accepts Jesus' canine metaphor and claims the same sort of benefit from Jesus that the centurion had asked for. In both cases, non-Jews are marginal in regard to Jesus' activity, yet that position involves them in the benefits of healing and/or exorcism. For Gentiles, words take the place of direct contact.

Jesus' Practice of Purity and His Commissioning of Apostles

Jesus' concern, as we have seen, was to address local Israel. Galilee might be the region of such communities, but so might the areas around the Decapolis on the eastern side of the Sea of Galilee, or the vicinity of Caesarea Philippi, or even Tyre and Sidon. In every case, Jesus went ahead on the supposition of the purity of those who heard him. His avoidance of urban centers, overt expressions of Roman hegemony and the ascendancy of Hellenistic culture, was the negative side of his positive acceptance of nonurban communities as genuine examples of Israel.

From his perspective, it was necessary to assert that such communities were clean until their actions proved them otherwise. That is precisely what Jesus did in a saying whose authenticity is widely accepted (Mark 7:14–15):

Hear me, all of you, and understand:
There is nothing outside the man, entering into him,
    which defiles him,
but those things coming out of the man are what defile
    him.

The conclusion of the "Jesus Seminar" is representative both of the conventional wisdom regarding the saying's authenticity and of what is usually done with the consensus. The saying is accepted as "a categorical challenge to the laws governing pollution and purity" and is attributed to Jesus.[24]

---

24. See R. W. Funk, R. W. Hoover, and the Jesus Seminar, *The Five Gospels: The Search for the Authentic Words of Jesus* (New York: Macmillan, 1993), 69.

All such interpretations ignore the issue of substance: the saying is an assertion *concerning* defilement, not a general denial of defilement. The assertion is easily construed in Aramaic attested from Jesus' period and place[25] and is more attractive when it is so rendered:

> *la' demin bar bar-'enasha'/da'teh bey demtamey*
> *bera' min da'tan min/bar-'enasha' 'elen demtamyey.*

The English representation might be:

> nothing that is outside a person/entering one defiles one,
> except that things coming from/a person, these defile one.

The slash (/) is used to help describe the poetics of the assertion, which divides into two lines, each of four beats followed by three beats. Using *bar* for "outside"[26] (in the phrase *demin bar*) produces a repetition of sound with "person" (*bar-'enasha'*). "Person" itself is repeated in the last line, so as to emphasize closure. The sound of *bar* is echoed in "except that" (*bera' min*),[27] linking the two lines by the same consonants that open the first line strikingly. The participle "defile" (from *tema'*)[28] dominates the sense of the entire saying; it is clearly an example of a *mashal*, the Hebrew term for a proverbial or parabolic teaching.

Rendering the aphorism into Aramaic obviously makes it no more and no less a saying of Jesus. That it can be so rendered, and is memorable in Aramaic, simply helps to confirm the suggestion that the circle of Jesus confronted the issue of defilement. The circle was centered in Galilee (without being limited to that region) and was characterized by fellowship at meals involving various people with different practices of purity. That description applies to the period of Jesus' own activity

---

25. See Joseph A. Fitzmyer and Daniel J. Harrington, *Manual of Palestinian Aramaic Texts*, Biblia et Orientalia 34 (Rome: Biblical Institute Press, 1978), where the forms here used are attested. The pointing, of course, is largely a matter of supposition on the basis of later texts, and a simplified scheme is recommended for that reason.

26. See ibid., 7.8.4.

27. See ibid., 29B.22.23. The result is that *min bar* appears in the first line and *bera' min* in the second.

28. I have used a form of the pael, of which the infinitive appears in ibid., 29B.20.15.

and also to the period after his death when the movement continued to engage in the practice of fellowship at meals. Before and after Jesus' death, the celebration of the kingdom's purity in such fellowship was the hallmark of the movement.

In either phase, the circle of Jesus needed to cope with the social issue of possible defilement as one member of Israel (with one set of practices) met another member of Israel (with a different set of practices). The Jesus Seminar uncritically accepts the present context of the saying, limited to a dispute about foods, as the generative concern of the saying.[29] If it is a *mashal* from the circle of Jesus, its setting cannot be determined from the literary context that later circles associated the aphorism with.

Had Jesus taken any other stance in regard to purity than the acceptance of each local community as Israel, he would have committed himself to engage in specific procedures of purification (such as John the Baptist's) prior to preaching the message of the kingdom.[30] His argument here in Mark 7:15 is as simple as an aphoristic assertion, just as his practice generally was straightforward: the purity of generic Israel is acknowledged as true purity. On that assumption, the promulgation of the kingdom by word and deed, by Jesus and by his disciples, could and should proceed. The statement concerning defilement represents a policy of treating all of Israel *as Israel*, pure by means of its customary practice.

The point of such sayings as Mark 7:15 (see also Matt. 15:11 and Luke 11:39–41) is that there is a link between integrity and cleanness: that Israelites are properly understood as pure and that what extends from a person, what he is and does and has, manifests that purity. Paul was to write some twenty-five years

---

29. For that reason, the version of the saying in *Thomas* (saying 14), which specifies what goes into "your mouth," is taken by the Jesus Seminar to be as original as what is in Mark. It seems much more likely that the setting in Luke (eating what is given you during missionary journeys [see Luke 10:8–9]) has influenced the working in *Thomas*. *Thomas* frequently gives the appearance of being a pastiche of materials from the Synoptic Gospels, together with other traditions. See Bruce D. Chilton, "The Gospel according to Thomas as a Source of Jesus' Teaching," in *Gospel Perspectives 5: The Jesus Tradition Outside the Gospels*, ed. D. Wenham (Sheffield, England: JSOT, 1985), 155–75.

30. See Bruce Chilton, "John the Purifier," in *Judaic Approaches to the Gospels*, International Studies in Formative Christianity and Judaism 2 (Atlanta: Scholars Press, 1994), 1–37.

later (and for his own purposes), "*Do you not know* that your body is a temple of the holy spirit within you, which you have from God?" (1 Cor. 6:19a, b). Paul may be alluding to a particular saying of Jesus' (see John 2:21) or to what he takes to be a theme of Jesus'; in either case, he refers his readers to what he assumes to be elementary knowledge of the gospel.

That Jesus and especially Paul (who identified himself as a Pharisee [see Phil. 3:5]) speak from such a perspective is not unusual. It is said that Hillel took a similar point of view and expressed it in a more heterodox manner. He defended an Israelite's right to bathe in Roman installations on the grounds that if Gentiles deem it an honor to wash the idols of their gods, Israelites should similarly deem it an honor (indeed, a duty) to wash their bodies, the image of God (Lev. Rab. 34.3). In other words, bathing does not make one pure but celebrates the fact of purity; in their quite different ways, Hillel and Paul demonstrate that representatives of the pharisaic movement — contrary to its repute in the Gospels — conceived of purity as a condition that Israelites could be assumed to enjoy, and out of which they should act. Fundamentally, Jesus' concern appears similarly to have been with cleanness as a matter of production rather than of consumption.

Jesus' perspective in regard to purity is attested within a passage that is also common to the Synoptics but that is particularly articulated in the source called Q. The source consists for the most part of distinct statements of Jesus, reflected best in some two hundred verses of Matthew and Luke that are not fully present in Mark. Q arranges the sayings of Jesus as if they were the teaching of a rabbi; it approximates to a mishnah, arranged by topic and the association of ideas and words.

In the commission to his twelve followers (and, in Luke, seventy followers) to preach and heal, Jesus specifically commands them to remain, until they depart, in whatever house receives them within a given village (Matt. 10:11; Mark 6:10; Luke 9:4; 10:7). That commandment by itself is a notable development compared with a pharisaic construction of purity because it presupposes that what the disciples eat, within any house that might receive them, is clean. Jesus' itineracy and that of his disciples, treated in much recent literature as if it were an obviously Graeco-Roman practice, was a profound and explicit statement of the general purity of food in Israel.

The mishnaic source called Q underscores that statement by having the disciples pronounce their peace upon the house in question (Matt. 10:12, 13; Luke 10:5, 6), and Luke's Jesus particularly insists that the disciples should eat what is set before them in whatever town they might enter (10:7, 8).[31] The pronouncement of peace and the injunction not to go from house to house within a given community (see Luke 10:7), but to stay put until the visit is over, had obvious utility within the missionary concerns of the mishnaic source. But the particular focus upon purity, all but obscured in Q with missionary directives, appears to have been Jesus'.

A last peculiarity of the commission in Q, one that has long seemed incomprehensible, finds its sense under our analysis. Although Mark's Jesus has the disciples without bread, bag, money, or a change of cloths, he *does* permit them a staff and sandals (6:8, 9). In the mishnaic source, however, just those obviously necessary items are singled out for *exclusion:* no staff should be carried, no sandals worn (cf. Matt. 10:9, 10; Luke 9:3; 10:4). The traditional attempt to explain differences within the lists as the result of missionary practices within the early Church is reasonable superficially, but that attempt only diverts attention from the obvious fact that the commission makes extremely poor sense as a missionary instrument. Why tell people not to take what on any journey they, practically speaking, would certainly need?

But if we understand the commission to treat every village they might enter as clean, as pure territory such as that in which sacrifice might be offered,[32] the perplexing feature of the commission makes eminent sense. The disciples are to enter villages exactly as pilgrims were to enter the Temple within pharisaic teaching: without the food, the sandals, the staffs, the garments, the bags, and the money (see Ber. 9:5; B. Yeb. 6b) that would nor-

---

31. *Thomas* saying 14 links just this injunction with the saying more primitively attested in Mark 7:15; Matt. 15:11. See n. 29 above.

32. Of course, within the pharisaic ethos, purity was held to be consistent with sacrifice, without any assumption that such purity would actually occasion sacrifice each time it was achieved.

mally accompany a journey. Q makes Jesus' commission into a
missionary discourse; within his ministry, it was designed to
be an enacted parable of Israel's purity.

Whether in the triply attested material of the Synoptics (a
probable reflection of Petrine tradition) or in the doubly attested
mishnaic source known as Q, a circle of concern associated with
Jesus is held to see purity as proceeding from Israel. Once one is
identified with Israel, it is not that which is without that defiles,
but those things that come from oneself. Separation from that
which is outside one does not therefore assure purity, and non-
Jews in the mixed environment of Galilee and the areas around
Galilee pose no particular danger to Israel. The circle of Jesus
frames its rhetoric for its specific, social circumstance of Israel
in the midst of the nations. Defilement here is a matter of fail-
ing to recognize the others of Israel, refusing to produce from
within and to contact on that basis the pure Israel that those
others represent.

Jesus' definition of Israel was unlike that of his followers
because it was not systematic. His policy of fellowship with
others of Israel, the assumption that their practices were to
be accepted as pure, implied that they were indeed Israel, but
there is no statement attributed (or attributable) to Jesus that
establishes the boundaries of Israel. Boundaries were precisely
among those things that were melting away in his eschatological imagination.

A characteristic claim is attested in the source of Jesus' sayings called Q:[33] "Many shall come from east and west and
recline in feasting with Abraham and Isaac and Jacob" (Matt.
8:11; Luke 13:28, 29). There can be no doubt of the emphasis
upon a future consummation in the saying, involving a particular (but unnamed) place, the actions and material of festivity
(including the luxurious custom of reclining, not sitting, at a

---

33. For a detailed analysis of the saying, see Bruce D. Chilton, *God in
Strength: Jesus' Announcement of the Kingdom* (Sheffield, England: Sheffield Academic Press, 1987), reprinted from Studien zum Neuen Testament und seiner
Umwelt 1 (Freistadt: Plöchl, 1979), 179–201. The significant differences between Matthew and Luke here show that Q was not the stable source some
scholars claim that it was.

banquet), and the incorporation of the many who shall rejoice in the company of the patriarchs.

Jesus' use of the imagery of feasting in order to refer to the kingdom, a characteristic of his message, is resonant both with early Judaic language of the kingdom and with his own ministry. The picture of God offering a feast on Mount Zion "for all peoples," where death itself is swallowed up, becomes an influential image from the time of Isa. 25:6–8. Notably, the Targum of Isaiah refers to the divine disclosure on Mount Zion that includes the image of the feast as "the kingdom of the LORD of hosts" (24:23).[34] Sayings such as the one cited from Q invoke that imagery, and Jesus' practice of fellowship at meals with his disciples and many others amounted to a claim that the ultimate festivity had already begun.

The development of systematic definitions of the Israel implied by the movement of Jesus became a necessity in the period after the resurrection. The two social forces that produced the necessity were (1) the acceptance of Jesus' message — including the claim he had been raised from the dead — among non-Jews, and (2) the increasing hostility of Jewish authorities, both the priesthood in Jerusalem and pharisaic leaders there and abroad. It is vital to appreciate, however, that those two forces of systematization, powerful as they were, were further developments of constitutional characteristics from the generative moment of the new movement: the movement of Jesus included more people in Israel than the movements around many other Judaic teachers at the time. His followers also claimed that their authority to do so exceeded other authorities. In their readiness to redefine "Israel," they perpetuated the substance of Jesus' policy of eschatological inclusion.

Jesus' Conflict with the Cultic Authorities in Jerusalem

Volume 1 of Christianity and Judaism — The Formative Categories has already introduced the nature of the conflict between

---

34. See the discussion in Chilton, *Galilean Rabbi,* 57–63.

Jesus and the authorities in the Temple.[35] Caiaphas, an unusually successful high priest, had decided to remove the council from its customary location within the buildings of the Temple to a site on the Mount of Olives called Ḥanuth ("marketplace" in Aramaic). At the same time, he permitted the vendors of sacrificial animals, who had usually conducted business at Ḥanuth, to set up shop within the great, outer court of the Temple. His reform incited Jesus (with his followers) to expel those vendors from the Temple with the use of force.

Jesus' decision to occupy the Temple is fully consistent with his usual practice of purity. By the time of the last period of his programmatic activity, in Jerusalem, he had already established the parabolic custom of joining with people in the villages of Galilee within the fellowship of meals that celebrated the kingdom. In his own practice, and in the practice of those disciples whom he commissioned to represent him, Jesus acknowledged the purity of generic Israel: those who produced what was consumed, forgiving and being forgiven as was appropriate, were fit for the fellowship of the kingdom.

Caiaphas's reform put an intermediary between what Israel produced and what was offered in sacrifice. In effect, what was acquired on the site was priests' produce that became one's own only by means of a commercial transaction. It interrupted the understanding that Israel was to appear before God in his Temple with what had been produced in Israel's own land and by Israel's own hands. Ultimately, Jesus' position prevailed because the normal understanding of rabbinic literature is that, both before and after Caiaphas, Ḥanuth (not the outer court) was the site of the vendors.[36]

In the time immediately after Jesus' occupation of the Temple, however, his position was tenuous. Although Jesus was momentarily protected by his popular following from action by the high priest and the security forces within the Temple, Caiaphas awaited an opportunity to condemn Jesus on grounds that

---

35. See Neusner and Chilton, *Revelation,* chap. 5, and Chilton *Temple of Jesus,* 91–111.

36. For further discussion, see Bruce Chilton, *A Feast of Meanings: Eucharistic Theologies from Jesus through Johannine Circles,* Supplements to *Novum Testamentum* 172 (Leiden: Brill, 1994), 75–81.

even the council would recognize. Jesus himself provided Caiaphas with the opportunity he sought. Eating and drinking with his followers in the context of his customary celebration of the kingdom, Jesus referred to the wine of fellowship as "blood" and to the bread of fellowship as "flesh." That is, he stated that the meal was more acceptable to God as sacrifice than what was done in Caiaphas's Temple.[37]

The charge of blasphemy that resulted in Jesus' execution was easily sustained (see Matt. 26:65 ‖ Mark 14:63). Once he claimed his meals were a better sacrifice than the conduct of the cult, he appeared to oppose the institution of the Temple, not merely the arrangements that Caiaphas preferred. Jesus was therefore denounced to the Romans as someone who undermined the legitimacy of the Temple that they themselves authorized. After all, sacrifice on behalf of the Romans and the emperor was offered in that Temple:[38] its smooth functioning was the image of the conviction that Roman hegemony was consistent with Judaic worship of the one true God. From the Roman as well as from the priestly point of view, Jesus' combined actions — occupying the Temple and claiming that his own meals were better than sacrifice there — amounted to blasphemy. He demeaned both the established authority of the Temple and the imperial assent to its operation.

Jesus could not have been unaware of the forces that he challenged by means of his actions. His assertion of the purity of Israel's produce over what the priests arranged to sell and his assertion of the superiority of his meals to the sacrifices that Rome underwrote were conscious (if not calculated) challenges of ordinary structures of authority. For that reason, we are drawn back to the narratives of Jesus' action within the Temple, in order to see what caused Jesus to act as he did.

Those narratives vary considerably from one another (see Matt. 21:12–13 ‖ Mark 11:15–17 ‖ Luke 19:45–46 ‖ John 2:13–17),[39]

---

37. See Bruce Chilton, "The Eucharist — Exploring Its Origins," *Bible Review* 110, no. 6 (December 1994): 36–43; a comprehensive treatment is available in Chilton, *Feast of Meanings.*

38. See Josephus, *The Jewish War* II, §409, and Philo, *The Embassy to Gaius,* 157, 317.

39. In addition, *Thomas* saying 64 is relevant to the issue.

but they agree on the central point that Jesus' purpose was to evict merchants from the Temple. Such an eviction is also envisaged in the book of Zechariah. There, as part of a climactic presentation of God's eschatological rule, the final verses insist that no trader is to have a place in the worship that is conducted in Jerusalem (Zech. 14:21).

The reason for their exclusion in Zechariah also sheds light on Jesus' motivation in occupying the Temple.[40] The vision in Zechariah 14 does not involve the punishment of merchants in themselves as being corrupt. Punishments are certainly envisaged in the chapter, but merchants are not singled out as a group worthy of such treatment. The point of the exclusion of the merchants is rather that everything within Jerusalem and Judah will belong to the LORD, so that sacrifice might be offered in ordinary implements (Zech. 14:20–21). Israel is to present of its own and with its own, precisely as in the teaching of Jesus. For Jesus as for the book of Zechariah in its final, compelling image, holiness is inconsistent with commercial trade.

Zechariah develops its vision of enhanced sanctity and purity at the end of time within the expectation of that day when "the LORD will become king over all the earth" (Zech. 14:9). Just as the question of what will become of Jerusalem and Judah becomes acute, so the issue of the rest of the nations is raised. The final chapter of Zechariah envisages the grievous punishment of those who come up against Jerusalem in a last, apocalyptic battle (Zech. 14:1–15). But then, in the same passage in which the exclusion of the traders is mentioned, the chapter and the book close with the specific mention of the requirement that those who survive of the nations should come to worship the LORD in Jerusalem during the Feast of Booths, year by year (14:16–21). The final note of Zechariah is one of inclusion.

In her recent study of the book of Zechariah, Katrina J. A. Larkin notes that the inclusion referred to at the end of the work in fact develops a theme introduced earlier.[41] She cites Zech.

---

40. More passages from Zechariah than are cited here are discussed in Chilton, *Temple of Jesus,* 135–36, 138, 145–46; and idem, *Feast of Meanings,* 114, 186–88, 191.

41. Katrina J. A. Larkin, *The Eschatology of Second Zechariah* (Kampen, Netherlands: Kok Pharos, 1994), 220.

8:22–23, where it is predicted that "many peoples and strong nations shall come to seek the Lord of hosts in Jerusalem." There is perhaps an even stronger link to the prediction in Zech. 2:11 that "many nations shall be joined to the Lord in that day." The connection of the verb "to join" (*lavah* in Hebrew) to the term "Levite" makes that statement appear all the more emphatic.[42] But however one decides the issue of the relative importance of passages, the point remains clear: Zechariah's vision, like Jesus' vision, includes the nations in the benefits that primarily are Israel's.

In the Aramaic translation of Zech. 14:9, where the Hebrew text refers to the Lord becoming king over all the earth, the Targum refers to the Lord's kingdom being revealed over all the dwellers of the earth. By means of a saying attributed to Rabbi Eliezer ben Hyrcanos, the association between the kingdom of God and the universal rule of which Zech. 14:9 speaks is attested within the first century.[43] Jesus' vision of the kingdom also involved Israel as the focus of God's activity, the place where the new purity of God's people would be answered by the powerful sanctity of God himself, claiming his own. But for Jesus as for the book of Zechariah, God's focus on Israel involved those around Israel, as either for or against the dawn of that light.

The story of the legion of demons establishes that the kingdom Jesus announces is inconsistent with the emphatic uncleanness of the maniac in the non-Jewish cemetery, the emphatically Roman territory, the unclean spirits themselves. It is not that he fears them, but that contact with him destroys what is unclean in them. The story asserts by means of its carefully chosen depiction of impurity that Jesus' representation of the divine kingdom dissolves every unclean thing that gets in its path, much as in the book of Zechariah the very flesh of those who attempt to lay siege to Jerusalem melts away at the appearance of the Lord (see Zech. 14:12).

The stories of the centurion and the Syrophoenician woman,

---

42. The point is not merely etymological; the words are associated in Num. 18:2.

43. For discussion, see Chilton, *Galilean Rabbi*, 67–68. Eliezer's statement is in the commentary on Exodus called the Mekhilta (17:14).

on the other hand, coordinate Jesus' activity with the alternative, inclusive aspect of Zechariah's expectation regarding non-Jews. The centurion is, in effect, like one of those described in Zech. 8:22, where the emphasis is upon the respectful entreaty of those from afar who seek out the LORD in Jerusalem. And Zech. 8:23, with its reference to those who will "take hold of the robe of a Jew" in their eagerness to seek God, represents an attitude much like that of the Syrophoenician woman.

Our conclusion is not intended to suggest that there is a direct link between the story of the legion and the destruction of the gentile armies in Zechariah 14, between the story of the centurion and the reference to the respectful nations in Zech. 8:22, or between the story of the Syrophoenician woman and the reference to the rude enthusiasm of the nations in Zech. 8:23. The point is rather that Jesus' understanding of purity is illuminated by the attitude developed in the book of Zechariah.

Within Israel, any form of priestly commercialism is to be replaced by the direct approach of Israel, its own produce immediately in hand. That is the vision of Zech. 14:20–21, a vision that was enacted in Jesus' occupation of the Temple. That new purity that occasioned the outbreak of God's sanctity, the rule of his kingdom, would destroy what was opposed to it and take up even sympathetic non-Jews (suitably respectful or not) in the recognition of its glory. Such is Jesus' warrant of God's intent for Israel, and at the same time his threat and promise to all who are not part of Israel.

6

The Israel of James,
the Community of Q,
and Peter

Israel within Jesus' activity is not a matter of definition but an imperative of transformation. Those who offer of their own, forgiving and being forgiven, join in that eschatological Israel that benefits even non-Jews. Jesus' position is difficult to compare with other definitions of Israel current in his period because he provided for no clear social structure. How are we to determine the difference between Jews and non-Jews, between those who are to engage in that eschatological transformation that constitutes Israel and those who are indirectly to benefit from it? And who knows whether a given non-Israelite is to be classed with the centurion and the Syrophoenician or with the demons and the pigs?

Jesus' focus on nonurban settlements of Jews assured that, as a theoretical or conceptual matter, the difference between Jews and others did not arise as an important issue. Such lines of demarcation had already been drawn by the time he or his followers contacted a village or town. He could proceed — for example in his commissioning of apostles to represent him — on the assumption of a collective understanding of communal identity. The same assumption resulted in his acceptance of local practices of purity as valid.

When generic purity was grossly violated, as in the case of the story of the legion, it was simply assumed that such impurity was inconsistent with Jesus' presence, and the story insists

118

that in any such confrontation, impurity will be eliminated. Within that generic concern with purity, collective agreement regarding who was marginal within the communal identity was validated, so that the centurion in Capernaum could be embraced without being touched. The Syrophoenician woman, however, signals the extension of the benefits of Israel beyond the realm of any purely local definition of what Israel is. Jesus' occupation of the Temple, especially within the context of his continuity with the book of Zechariah, confirms the force of his conviction of Israel's fitness for worship and of the benefit of such worship beyond the limits of Jerusalem, Judah, even Israel as usually understood.

The position of Jesus' followers after his crucifixion differed from his own. Jerusalem had become a focus of the movement; it was the first urban center among many. The new environment involved a greater variety of people who claimed to represent Israel and a greater variety of people who were at odds with any definition of Israel. A conceptual, social definition of what Israel was and should be became necessary for Jesus' movement to negotiate its way among the options that groups such as priests, Pharisees, and Essenes offered. At the same time, because the movement was frequently under pressure from the definitions of other groups, Jesus' followers needed to define themselves in relation to those competing definitions of Israel.

The three stories considered in the last chapter derive from cycles of tradition that have already been identified. The present concern is to explain how each of the communities that produced and maintained its own cycle of tradition framed a definition of Israel, in relation both to those outside Israel and to those who claimed to be within. The order of presentation will be as in the last chapter, beginning with the circle of James, moving through the community of Q, and ending with the circle of Peter. That order is not chronological; indeed, from the point of view of dating, we should move in the opposite sequence. Because our concern is with the definition of Israel, we move from the strictest model of Israel as centered on the Temple (in the circle of James), through the reflection of severe tension within Israel as a result of Jesus' movement (in Q), and on to the conviction that God's spirit is available through Christ to those outside Israel as well as to those within (in the circle of Peter).

The Circle of James

The importance of James as a central authority within the primitive stage of Christianity has already been discussed in volume 1 of Christianity and Judaism — The Formative Categories. The sources of that discussion were principally Acts and Galatians, which were cited in order to explain James's approach to Scripture. A passage within the Gospels will be the focus of attention here, in order to elucidate James's conception of Israel itself, which was a function of his attitude toward the Temple. In order to lay the groundwork for a consideration of James's concern for the Temple, we begin with the description of James provided by Hegesippus, a Christian writer from the second century.

Hegesippus — as cited by Eusebius (see *History* 2.23.1–18) — characterizes James, Jesus' brother, as the person who exercised immediate control of the church in Jerusalem. Although Peter had initially gathered a group of Jesus' followers in Jerusalem, his interests and activities further afield left the way open for James to become the natural head of the community there. That change, and political changes in Jerusalem itself (detailed in the next section, on the community of Q), made the Temple the effective center of the local community of Jesus' followers. James practiced a careful and idiosyncratic purity in the interests of worship in the Temple. He abstained from wine and animal flesh, did not cut his hair or beard, and forsook oil and bathing. According to Hegesippus, those special practices and his linen garments gave him access even to the sanctuary. Josephus reports he was killed in the Temple in 62 at the instigation of the high priest Ananus during the interregnum of the Roman governors Festus and Albinus (*Antiquities* 20.9.1 §§197–203). Hegesippus gives a more circumstantial, less politically informed, account of the martyrdom.

In addition to the sort of close association with the Temple that could and did result in conflict with the authorities there, the circle of James is expressly claimed in Acts to have exerted authority as far away as Antioch, by means of emissaries who spoke Greek (Acts 15:13–35). The particulars of the dispute (with both Pauline and Petrine understandings of purity) will not detain us here, because they have been discussed at some length in volume 1. What is of immediate import is that James alone determines the outcome of apostolic policy. James in Acts agrees that Gentiles who turn to God are not to be encumbered with needless regulations (15:19), and yet he insists they be instructed by letter to abstain "from the pollutions of idols, and from fornication, and from what is strangled, and from blood" (v. 20).

The grounds given for the Jacobean policy are that the law of Moses is commonly acknowledged (Acts 15:21); the implication is that to disregard such elemental considerations of purity as James specifies would be to dishonor Moses. Judas Barsabbas and Silas are then dispatched with Paul and Barnabas to deliver the letter in Antioch along with their personal testimony (vv. 22–29) and are said particularly to continue their instruction as prophets (vv. 32, 33). They refer to the regulations of purity as necessities (v. 28), and no amount of Lukan gloss can conceal that what they insist upon is a serious challenge of Paul's position (cf. 1 Corinthians 8).

James's devotion to the Temple is also reflected in Acts 21. When Paul arrives in Jerusalem, James and the presbyters with him express concern at the rumor that Paul is telling Jews who live among the Gentiles not to circumcise. Their advice is for Paul to demonstrate his piety by purifying himself, paying the expenses of four men under a vow, and entering the Temple with them (Acts 21:17–26). The result is a disastrous misunderstanding. Paul is accused of introducing "Greeks" into the Temple, a riot ensues, and Paul himself is arrested (21:27–36). James is not mentioned again in Acts, but Hegesippus's description shows his devotion to the Temple did not wane.

Within the Gospels, certain passages reflect the exceptional devotion of James's circle to the Temple. The best example is Mark 7:6–13 (and, with an inverted structure, Matt. 15:3–9); although the topic of the chapter overall is purity, the issue assumed in the passage itself is the sanctity of the Temple in particular (Mark 7:10–13). The issue is spelled out in terms of a dispute concerning *qorban,* the Aramaic term for a cultic gift (Mark 7:11).

The dispute reflects Jesus' own stance that what is owed to one's parents cannot be sheltered by declaring it dedicated to the Temple. The crucial point of such a gambit of sheltering is that one might continue to use the property *after* its dedication to the Temple, while what was given to a person would be transferred forthwith.[1] The basic complaint about the practice, especially as stated in the simple epigram of Mark 7:11–12, derives from Jesus. The complaint is characteristic of him; quite aside from his occupation of the Temple, he criticized commercial arrangements there (see Matt. 17:24–27; Mark 12:41–44; Luke 21:1–4).

The dominical epigram has here been enveloped in a much more elaborate argument, crafted within the circle of James. Mark 7:6–13 is a syllogism, developed by means of scriptural terms of reference. Isaiah's complaint (29:13) frames the entire argument: the people claim to honor God, but their heart is as far from him as their vain worship, rooted in human commandments (Mark 7:6b–7). That statement is related in Mark 7:10–12 to the tradition of *qorban,* taken as an invalidation of the Mosaic prescription to honor parents. The simple and unavoidable conclusion is that the tradition violates the command of God (Mark 7:8–9, 13).

The argument as it stands insists upon the integrity of the Temple and the strict regulation of conduct there; it attacks opponents for too little concern for the Temple, not too much. At the same time, the passage presents Jesus as maintaining a literal loyalty to the Scriptures that the Pharisees — and Jesus himself — did not. (The actual form of citation, moreover, is derived from the Greek translation of the Hebrew Bible, the Septuagint. That is a sign of the Hellenistic phase of the cycle of tradition that James inspired.) Those aspects of the presentation of Jesus' saying are typical of the circle of James.

---

1. See Ernst Bammel, "Gottes ΔIAΘHKH (Gal. III.15–17) und das jüdische Rechtdenken," *New Testament Studies* 6 (1959/1960): 313–19; Zeev W. Falk, "Notes and Observations on Talmudic Vows," *Harvard Theological Review* 159 (1966): 309–12.

Regular worship in the Temple became a characteristic feature of Jesus' movement only after the crucifixion and resurrection. Before then, as we have seen in the last chapter, Jesus'
conflict with the cultic authorities over the most basic issues
of how offerings should be brought to the Temple resulted in
deadly opposition to him. But one of the most surprising developments of the period after that time is that a group of Jesus'
followers continued to reside in Jerusalem and that worship
in the Temple was one of their primary purposes there. The
removal of Caiaphas from the high priesthood (discussed in
the next section) and the consequent reversal of his reforms
(to which Jesus himself had objected) fed the conviction of
Jesus' followers that he who had been crucified had also been
vindicated.

Acts pictures Peter as the first leader of a tightly knit group,
which broke bread at home and held property in common as
well as worshiping in the Temple (see Acts 1:12–26; 2:46; 3:1–
26; 4:1–37). But Peter is also represented as active much further
afield (see the section below entitled "Peter"). A shift in leadership of the community in Jerusalem, from Peter to James,
became necessary, and Acts clearly attests it (see Act 12:17).

Acts 12:17 also reflects an important (and overlooked) aspect
of the shift in power from Peter to James. Peter has been im-
prisoned at the command of Herod Agrippa and is delivered
by means of an angel. Greeted by companions in the house he
goes to, he orders them to tell James of his release and departs
to an unspecified place. Peter had aroused priestly opposition in
a way James did not (see Acts 4:1–31; 5:12–42), and the priests
were able to use their influence with Herod. In contrast, James
managed to adapt Jesus' message to a greater devotion to the
Temple than most Jews demonstrated. Just that devotion is reflected in the scriptural syllogism regarding *qorban*, as well as
in Hegesippus's description of James.

The syllogism in regard to *qorban* also assumes that devotion to Jesus' teaching is consistent with greater loyalty to the
Temple. Hegesippus's account of the death of James conveys the
same assumption in its reference to the attempt by a member of
a priestly family to save James from death in the last moments
of his life. Indeed, the entire scene of his martyrdom unfolds in

the context of the Temple at the time of Passover and reflects the particular devotion of James's circle both to that feast and to the conduct of sacrificial worship in the Temple.[2]

Typically, the circle of James applied the Scriptures directly to the situation of Jesus' followers, on the understanding of their regulative authority. We saw in volume 1 (pp. 118–23) how James cited the reference of Amos to the restoration of the house of David (in Amos 9:11–12). As James develops the meaning of Amos in Acts 15:16–21, the Gentiles are to recognize the triumph of David, and that implies that they are to remain Gentiles. They are not a part of Israel, although they are to keep basic rules of purity in order to honor the law of Israel.

James's focus was on Jesus' role as the ultimate arbiter within the Davidic line, and there was never any question in his mind but that the Temple was the natural place to worship God and acknowledge Jesus. Embracing the Temple as central meant for James, as it meant for everyone associated with worship there, maintaining the purity that it was understood that God required in his house and keeping it better than many of those associated with the priesthood. That is the point of the scriptural syllogism regarding *qorban*. According to James, Jesus' purity involved excluding Gentiles, even those who acknowledged some rudiments of purity out of loyalty to the Mosaic law, from the interior courts of the Temple. There, only Israel was to be involved in sacrifice, and followers of Jesus were to accept particular responsibility for such sacrifice (so Acts 21:17–36). The line of demarcation between Israel and non-Israel was no invention within the circle of James, but a natural result of seeing Jesus as the triumphant scion of the house of David.

Peter's imprisonment by Herod Agrippa can be dated rather precisely to 44 C.E.[3] By that time, then, James had emerged as a prominent authority, the natural leader of the group in Jerusalem. Earlier, in reference to his visit to Jerusalem in 35 C.E., Paul refers to meeting Peter and James, but he alludes to receiv-

---

2. See Bruce Chilton, *A Feast of Meanings: Eucharistic Theologies from Jesus through Johannine Circles,* Supplements to *Novum Testamentum* 172 (Leiden: Brill, 1994), 93–108.

3. See C. K. Barrett, *The Acts of the Apostles,* International Critical Commentary (Edinburgh: T. and T. Clark, 1994), 592.

ing instruction only from Peter (see Gal. 1:18–19).[4] During the
intervening period, ca. 40 C.E., the circle of James promulgated
its own instructional gospel, comparable to Peter's and building upon it. That was the basis of James's authority, which the
Apostolic Council reflected in Acts 15 confirmed. That council
is usually dated in 49 C.E. When Judas Barsabbas and Silas were
sent by the council to deliver its judgment (which was originally
James's opinion) in Antioch, it authorized James's version of the
gospel to be delivered in Greek. When Acts 15:32–33 refers to
Judas and Silas as prolonging their visit in Antioch after they
had read the letter from the council, we are given a glimpse into
the process by which materials originally framed in Aramaic
were rendered into Greek. At that moment, the importance of
non-Jewish testimony to Jesus *within its own environment* (rather
than within Israel) was emphasized. The sequel to the story of
the legion, in which the restored maniac is portrayed as preaching among his own people (Mark 5:18–20), is an example of that
development.

At the same time, we are shown how James's classic understanding of Israel was considered authoritative, even for the
largely non-Jewish congregation in Antioch. Here, in the place
where Jesus' followers were first called "Christians" (so Acts
11:26),[5] it is accepted after a considerable controversy that, although Gentiles may not be required to circumcise, neither may
they be considered one with Israel. James's Israel consisted of
those who recognized Jesus, the scion of the Davidic line, as the
guardian of true, noncommercial purity in the Temple.

The Community of Q

The source called Q, which might be described as the mishnah
of Jesus, presents its earliest material in a way that makes it
possible to understand Jesus' own preaching.[6] The compilation

---

4. See Chilton, *Feast of Meanings*, 81–82, 110.
5. See Barrett, *Acts of the Apostles*, 556–57.
6. For a recent, sound treatment (which corrects some excesses of North
American discussion), see David Catchpole, *The Quest for Q* (Edinburgh: T.
and T. Clark, 1993).

of that mishnah in Aramaic ca. 35 C.E. occurred in circumstances that were generally favorable to the preservation of Jesus' message within an oral environment. In the year 36, Caiaphas himself was removed from office (together with Pilate, his protector) by the Syrian legate Vitellius (so Josephus, *Antiquities* 18 §§90–95).[7] His innovation of installing vendors in the Temple cannot have survived his removal, so that disciples of Jesus had access to a better regulated Temple than Jesus did (from their point of view), and there is no reason to suppose they could not have circulated freely in Judaea and Galilee, as Q supposes they should.

But the composition of Q in its Syrian phase, a decade later, presupposes a significant rejection of the message of Jesus.[8] The eschatological woes pronounced against Chorazin, Bethsaida, and Capernaum (Luke 10:13–15), for example, reflect the refusal of Jesus' emissaries.[9] During Jesus' own ministry, Capernaum had provided a model of success (see Luke 4:23); its later resistance — along with more prominent cities such as Bethsaida — provoked a bitter reaction. Deprived of the hospitality that would have been a mark of the acceptance of their message, the community of Q wore their poverty as a badge of honor. Out of this situation there arose the virtual equation between poverty and the kingdom that is such a strong feature of several sayings, especially the first beatitude, "Blessed are the poor, because the kingdom of God is yours" (Luke 6:20).

The blessing of the poor is linked to a scenario in which the rich are to suffer. Moreover, the poor are associated with those who are abused "for the sake of the son of man," and the rich are associated with those who embraced the false prophets of

---

7. At the same time, Vitellius released the high-priestly vestments from custody in the Roman fortress adjacent to the Temple known as the Antonia. For further discussion, see Bruce Chilton, *The Temple of Jesus: His Sacrificial Program within a Cultural History of Sacrifice* (University Park: Pennsylvania State University Press, 1992) 107–9.

8. In accord with the usual practice, the citation of Luke here presupposes that the Matthean form of the material is also in view.

9. See the discussion in Catchpole, *Quest for Q*, 171–76, and Leif E. Vaage, *Galilean Upstarts: Jesus' First Followers according to Q* (Valley Forge, Pa.: Trinity Press International, 1994), 108, 117.

old (Luke 6:20–26). The social situation could hardly be plainer, as David Catchpole has observed:

> Here, then, by employing the language of opposition which, however, falls short of separation, and by building on earlier use of the deuteronomic pattern of perpetually persecuted prophets, which had been employed (as it were) domestically within Israel the editor allows us a glimpse of a situation within the community of Israel.[10]

Tension is rising in Israel, as a result of the attempt after the resurrection to implement Jesus' commission of twelve disciples to represent him. Jesus is now understood as "the son of man," a phrase that in Catchpole's words "conveys the heavenly status and future coming in judgment of the Jesus who had been known on earth."[11] That keen sense of what the future is to bring, the reversal in standing of oppressor and oppressed, developed into the apocalyptic assurance that also characterizes Q. The community of Q know they are the "little flock" to whom the kingdom has been given; only a brief interval separates them from their reward (Luke 12:32). The judgment of the kingdom is to be as severe as Q's parable of the returning king (Luke 19:11–27).[12]

Reference has already been made in the last chapter to Jesus' promise of the inclusion of many from east and west in the patriarchal feast of the kingdom (Matt. 8:11–12; Luke 13:28–29). The mishnaic source of which that saying was part is marked by a tendency to be pointed against the Jewish opponents of the movement. In the Matthean version, the saying appears as an addendum to the healing of the servant of the Roman centurion, and with an explicit warning against "the sons of the kingdom" (8:12). In the Lukan version, the saying is presented as part of a discourse concerning salvation in which

---

10. Catchpole, *Quest for Q*, 94. The entire discussion, pp. 81–94, should be required reading for those who assume that any reference to poverty can only have come from Jesus; see Vaage, *Galilean Upstarts*, 56–57, 107.

11. Catchpole, *Quest for Q*, 94.

12. Of course, there may be dominical elements in the sayings mentioned here (e.g., Luke 12:31; Matt. 6:33). But in their present form, they tell us more about the community of Q than about Jesus.

hearers are warned that merely having enjoyed Jesus' company during his lifetime is no guarantee of fellowship with the patriarchs in the eschatological feast (13:22–30). The differences between the two versions make the supposition of a fixed, written Q appear implausible at this point and commend the model of an instructional source — susceptible to local variation — for those who wished to teach in Jesus' name. Q is best seen as a mishnah for those who wished to follow the pattern of the twelve disciples whom Jesus had commissioned as his representatives.

Despite the differences between the versions of Q represented by Matthew and by Luke, respectively, the two Gospels commonly reflect how the saying was developed between the time of Jesus and the composition of the source of instructions. Jesus' teaching, as we have seen in the last chapter, focused on those who would come from east and west, marginal in relation to Israel or even outside Israel, in order to join in the benefits of the feast of the kingdom with Abraham, Isaac, and Jacob. That would have been how his position was remembered around 35 C.E., when what we call Q, a mishnah in Jesus' name, began to circulate among Jesus' more prominent followers. Then, however, the experience of resistance to the message that Jesus had commissioned the Twelve to deliver to Israel caused a new note of bitterness to be sounded. "Weeping and gnashing of teeth" was promised to those in Israel who refused to accept the message of the kingdom, and their place at the table of the kingdom was understood to be handed over to those who had been marginal or excluded.[13]

In order to appreciate the position of the community that composed Q, it is vital to understand that the punishment of those in Israel who rejected Jesus was part of an apocalyptic expectation of judgment. What was threatened to particular places that should have embraced the message of Jesus and did not (such as Chorazin and Bethsaida [see Luke 10:13]) was also in store for "this generation" of unresponsive Jews as a

---

13. For a more technical discussion of the evolution of the saying, see Bruce D. Chilton, *God in Strength: Jesus' Announcement of the Kingdom* (Sheffield, England: Sheffield Academic Press, 1987), reprinted from Studien zum Neuen Testament und seiner Umwelt 1 (Freistadt: Plöchl, 1979), 179–201.

whole (see Luke 11:31–32, 47–51). "The twelve tribes of Israel" were themselves to be judged by those faithful to Jesus (Luke 22:28–30); descent from Abraham could not be claimed as an unconditional privilege in the eschatological accounting (Luke 3:7–9).

The apocalyptic imagination of Q takes it to the very limit of a classic definition of Israel, such as is represented by the circle of James. The experience of rejection entailed hardship because the practice mandated by Jesus involved living in communities of Jews on the basis of their hospitality. An inhospitable Israel was to have the very dust of its streets shaken off the disciples' feet (see Luke 10:11), but widespread or persistent inhospitality would obviously constitute a serious challenge to the very existence of Jesus' movement. Q represents a response to that challenge. Those who preached in the name of Jesus around 45 C.E. could count on the support of only certain communities, some of them in Syria, and their attitude toward "Israel" as usually understood was ambivalent.

On the one hand, as a result of the experience of the rejection of Jesus' message, some in Israel are threatened with eschatological judgment. On the other hand, the assumption that Israel is truly the focus of the kingdom's disclosure means that the message must still be directed there, whether it is accepted or not. The usurpation by outsiders of the place of those in Israel who have rejected the message of Jesus' representatives is here a matter of the judgment that is to come, not an accomplished fact in the life of the community. Q is interested less in social constitution than in final justice. The result is that it comes to the brink of replacing Israel with a new model, the Church, without actually doing so.

Peter

Peter shared with Jesus the hope of a climactic disclosure of divine power, signaled in the willingness of nations to worship on Mount Zion. That hope is certainly attested within Judaic sources extant by the first century. Chief among them, from the point of view of its influence upon the New Testament, is the book of Zechariah. Zechariah provided the point of departure for Jesus' inclusive program of purity and forgiveness as the occasions of the kingdom. Jesus is said to have mentioned the prophet by name (see Matt. 23:34–36; Luke 11:49–51).

The book programmatically concerns the establishment of restored worship in the Temple, especially at the Feast of Sukkoth (14:16–19). "All the nations" are to go up to Jerusalem annually for worship (v. 16), and the transformation of which that worship is part involves the provision of "living waters" from the city (v. 8, cf. John 4:10, 14). That image is related to an earlier "fountain opened for the house of David and the inhabitants of Jerusalem in view of sin and uncleanness" (13:1). Here we see the association of forgiveness and purity that is a feature of Jesus' program, as well as the notion of an immediate release, without any mention of sacrifice, from what keeps Israel from God. God himself is held to arrange the purity he requires, so that the sacrifice he desires might take place.

Zechariah features the commissioning of a priest (chap. 3; see Matt. 16:18, 19), an oracle against swearing (5:3, 4; see Matt. 5:33–37), a vision of a king humbly riding an ass (9:9; see Matt. 21:1–9; Mark 11:1–10; Luke 19:28–40; John 12:12–19), the prophetic receipt of thirty shekels of silver in witness against the owners of sheep (11:4–17; see Matt. 26:14–16; 27:3–10; cf. Mark 14:10, 11; Luke 22:3–6). It is obvious that the connections between Jesus' ministry and Zechariah do not amount to a common agenda, and Matthew clearly reflects a tendency to increase the fit between the two. But the similarities are suggestive of Jesus' appropriation of Zechariah's prophecy of eschatological purity, as a final, more fundamental connection would indicate. As we have seen in the last chapter, the climactic vision of Zechariah insists that every vessel in Jerusalem will belong to the LORD and become a fit vessel for sacrifice. As part of that insistence, the text asserts that no trader will be allowed in the Temple (14:20, 21). In the light of Zechariah, Jesus' occupation of the Temple appears an enactment of prophetic purity in the face of a commercial innovation, a vigorous insistence that God would prepare his own people and vessels for eschatological worship.

Peter perpetuated that vision by means of his fidelity both

to breaking bread at home with the disciples and in worship within the Temple (see Acts 2:42–47).[14] The common owner- ship of possessions in Jerusalem, which is emphasized in the description of Petrine practice (in addition to Acts 2:44–45, see 4:32–5:11), also has its roots in the Zecharian vision. Common- ality of goods in the vicinity of the Temple presupposed the principle that no buying or selling would be at issue; it was in applying just that principle that Jesus went to his death. At the same time, Acts portrays Peter's activity much farther afield; he is active in Samaria (8:14–25), Lydda (9:32–35), Joppa (9:36– 43), and Caesarea (10:1–48; 12:19). Paul refers, as if as a matter of course, to Peter's presence personally in Antioch (see Gal. 2:11–14), and by the time of the pseudepigraphic 1 Peter (writ- ten around C.E. 90) he is pictured as writing from Rome with Silvanus (see 1 Peter 5:12–13) to churches in the north of Asia Minor (1:1, 2). If, then, Jerusalem was a center for Peter in the way it was not for Jesus, it was certainly not a limit of his op- erations. Rather, the Temple appears to have featured as the hub of a much wider network of contacts that linked Jews from abroad and even Gentiles (see Acts 10:1–48; 11:1–18, 15:1–11; and Gal. 2:1–14) in common recognition of a new, eschatological fellowship defined by the teaching of Jesus.

The key to the connection between Peter's residence in Jeru- salem and his activity in Syria and beyond is provided by the vision that he relates as the warrant for his visit to the house of Cornelius, the Roman centurion (Acts 10:1–48). Peter is praying on a rooftop in Joppa around noon. His vision occurs while he is hungry and concerns a linen lowering from heaven, filled with four-footed animals, reptiles, and birds. A voice says, "Arise, Peter, slaughter and eat," and he refuses (in words rem- iniscent of Ezek. 4:14). But a voice again says, "What God has cleansed, you will not defile" (see Acts 10:9–16).

Peter defends his baptisms in the house of Cornelius on the basis of his vision in the course of a dispute with those who ar- gued that circumcision was a requirement of adherence to the movement (Acts 11:1–18). He also cites his activity among non-

---

14. For further discussion and an analysis of the influence of that pattern upon the Petrine version of eucharist, see Chilton, *Feast of Meanings,* 75–92.

Jews at a later point, in the context of what has come to be called
the Apostolic Council (Acts 15:7–11). Throughout, the position
of Peter appears to have been consistent: God may make, and
has made, eschatological exceptions to the usual practice of purity. Those exceptions include the acceptance of uncircumcised
men in baptism and fellowship with them.

Considerable attention was devoted, in the first volume of
this series, to the confrontation in which Peter was involved
with Paul at Antioch (reflected in Galatians 2). From the point
of view of both Paul and James, Peter's behavior there was inconsistent. His commitment to fellowship caused him at first to
join in Paul's habit of eating together with non-Jews, but the
arrival of some people from James's group caused him then to
withdraw from such fellowship (Gal. 2:12). Neither James nor
Paul, however, did Peter justice.

James, as we have seen, urged a classic definition of Israel upon the followers of Jesus. Paul (as treated in volume 1,
and discussed again in the next chapter) experimented with
a radically new definition: Israel consists of those who believe in Christ Jesus. But Peter appears not to have engaged
in such questions of conceptual definition. Israel might remain Israel, under the normal understanding, but God's spirit
could also extend to non-Jews and justify their baptism (Acts
10:47). The same sort of conceptual silence in regard to Israel
that is characteristic of Jesus' theology is also evident within
Peter's.

We saw in volume 1 that Peter's emphasis upon the importance of spirit determined his attitude toward the Scriptures of
Israel. In the Transfiguration, for example, Jesus stands side by
side with Moses and Elijah; the son of God and the prophetic
covenant together mediate God's own spirit. But social policy
is left undefined under Peter's approach. According to Acts 15,
Peter concluded on the basis of God's gift of the spirit to Gentiles that they could not be required to be circumcised (Acts
15:6–11). On the other hand, Paul shows in Galatians 2 that
Peter was not willing to make a general principle for or against
Mosaic requirements and that he could change his mind when
confronted with differing interpretations and practices. But his
apparent ambivalence reflects a commitment to the twin loyal-

ties of a single son and a single law, together mediating the same spirit.

Despite the consistency of Peter's position with Jesus', it could not serve as a practical guide in framing a social identity for the followers of Jesus after the resurrection. The policy of taking Israel as one found it was wise in the case of Jesus, owing to the cultural and geographical limitation of his ministry. But as soon as his movement extended beyond the land — and more especially beyond the culture — of what was commonly agreed to be Israel, that policy could be portrayed as intellectually bankrupt and morally inconsistent. Was a group of non-Jewish believers who accepted baptism an example of Israel or not? The strength of the positions of James and Paul was that they provided a clear answer to that question, where Peter did not.

The two greatest intellectual leaders of the Church in the primitive phase were Paul and James. Their framing of coherent answers to the question of Israel is an index of their rigor and analytic power. But their brilliance did not permit them to eclipse the influence of Peter. In the next chapter, we will see how Peter's apparent incoherence came to guide early Christians to an understanding of the relationship between Church and Israel that is neither Pauline nor Jacobean.

7

The Synoptic Gospels, Paul, Hebrews, and Revelation: Practicing the Body of Christ

The principal cycles of tradition that stand behind the Synoptic Gospels were contributed by the circles that we have already considered: groups defined by their loyalty to Peter, or to James, or to the mishnaic authority of Q. In addition, there was a revision of the Jacobean cycle, promulgated in Greek by Joseph Barsabbas and Silas in Antioch after the council around 49 C.E. (see Acts 15:22–33). After 70 C.E., "the little apocalypse" (reflected in Mark 13 and its parallels), a Syrian addition to the Jacobean revision, was composed; it is a response to James's martyrdom and the Temple's destruction.[1]

These cycles were amalgamated into a curriculum for those preparing for baptism in Jesus' name within the many Hellenistic cities where churches emerged. The very name for "church" in Greek, *ekklesia*, reflects the consciousness of a people who see themselves as "called out" (from *ek* and *kaleo* in Greek) from their surroundings. The term is used in ordinary, secular Greek to refer to an assembly of people summoned for a purpose,[2] and it is applied in the book of Acts both to the congregation

---

1. The likely compiler was Silas, who under a more current form of his name (Silvanus) was involved in several sorts of apocalyptic speculation (cf. 1 Thess. 1:1; 2 Thess. 1:1; 1 Pet. 5:12). For further discussion, see Chilton, *Feast of Meanings*, 150–56.

2. See Henry George Liddel and Robert Scott, *A Greek-English Lexicon* (Oxford: Clarendon, 1901), 435.

of the Israelites whom Moses led out to the wilderness (Acts 7:38) and to the congregation of Jesus' followers in Jerusalem who were subject to persecution (Acts 8:1). The term appears some 114 times in the New Testament and is by far the most common designation of Christian groups, whether considered as the local assembly or as a single movement.[3]

The Barnaban Policy

Those who were called out from their usual activities for baptism required a concentrated education in the life of faith; after all, many of those who were attracted to the teaching of Jesus had had no prior background in Judaism and had received no specific information in regard to Jesus himself. The first ecumenical catechesis of the primitive Church, developed originally in Antioch, is reflected in the Synoptic Gospels. The most likely exponent of the unified catechesis is Barnabas, as is discussed in volume 1 of *Christianity and Judaism — The Formative Categories* (chap. 6). His standing is quite consistent with the wide acceptance of the Synoptic tradition. The greater accommodation to Jacobean influence in the Synoptics as compared to Paul is also explained by the influence of Barnabas (see Gal. 2:13).

The Synoptic catechesis was a paradigm that was then developed and published in Rome (Mark, ca. 71 C.E.), Damascus (Matthew, ca. 80 C.E.), and Antioch itself (Luke, ca. 90 C.E.). The spine of each Gospel is the narrative catechesis of the Petrine cycle, supplemented by the instruction of the Twelve (Q), the Jacobean revision of material, and the apocalyptic addendum of Joseph Barsabbas and Silas. Similarities and differences among the Synoptic Gospels are best understood as functions of the particular sort of catechesis — systematic preparation of catechumens — that was current in each community. No Gospel is

---

3. For a full discussion, see K. L. Schmidt, "Ekklesia," in *Theological Dictionary of the New Testament*, ed. G. Kittel, trans. G. W. Bromiley (Grand Rapids: Eerdmans, 1978), 501–36; P. T. O'Brien, "Church," in *Dictionary of Paul and His Letters*, ed. G. F. Hawthorne and R. P. Martin (Downers Grove, Ill.: InterVarsity, 1993), 123–31.

simply a copy of another; rather, each represents the choices among varying traditions, written and/or oral, and the development of those traditions that had taken place in a given locality.[4]

Barnabas is blamed by Paul in Galatians for being taken up in the "hypocrisy" of Peter and the "rest of the Jews," Peter's hypocrisy being that he had separated from the company of Gentiles he had formally eaten with (Gal. 2:11–13). Peter's position, as we saw in the last chapter, was in fact a function of his conviction that God's spirit in baptism overcame the impurity of non-Jews, without abrogating God's choice of Israel. Barnabas can be expected to have been more rigorous than Peter in regard to questions of purity and impurity. As a Levite from Cyprus (Acts 4:36), he had an awareness of what it meant to live with priestly concerns in a Hellenistic environment. His devotion to the Petrine understanding of pure worship is marked by his willingness to sell off his property in order to join the group in Jerusalem (Acts 4:37).

Barnabas, then, was associated with Peter before he was associated with Paul, so that Paul's attempt (as reflected in Galatians) to claim Barnabas's loyalty in opposition to Peter had little chance of success. After all, it was Barnabas's introduction that brought Paul into contact with the apostles in Jerusalem, despite Paul's well-deserved reputation as an enemy of the movement (Acts 9:27–30). Whatever disagreements might have stood between James and Barnabas, Barnabas enjoyed the implicit trust of the church in Jerusalem. When followers of Jesus from Cyprus and Cyrene preached to non-Jews in Antioch and enjoyed success, Barnabas was commissioned to investigate (see Acts 11:19–26). It was during the course of a sojourn that lasted over a year that Barnabas introduced Paul to Antioch.

Adherents of the movement came to be known as "Christians" (meaning partisans of Christ) in Antioch, and they embraced that term of intended ridicule.[5] The use of the term

---

4. For further explanation, see Bruce Chilton, *Profiles of a Rabbi: Synoptic Opportunities in Reading about Jesus*, Brown Judaic Studies 177 (Atlanta: Scholars Press, 1989).

5. For a cautious discussion, see C. K. Barrett, *The Acts of the Apostles*, The International Critical Commentary (Edinburgh: T. and T. Clark, 1994), 556.

by outsiders highlights the marginal status of non-Jews who accepted baptism. Without conversion to Judaism, they were not Jews in the usual understanding; having rejected the gods of Hellenism by being baptized, they were also no longer representative of the Graeco-Roman syncretism that was then fashionable. By calling disciples *Christiani*, a term analogous to *Caesariani* and *Augustiniani*, outsiders compared the movement more to a political faction than to a religion. It would be as if, in English, we called a disciple a "Christite," on the model of Thatcherite, Reaganite, Clintonite, and so on.

Acts describes Barnabas in the context of his visit in Antioch as "a good man, full of holy spirit and faith" (Acts 11:24). The reference to the spirit attests his connection with the Petrine understanding of discipleship that he had fully accepted. Unlike Peter, however, Joseph called Barnabas was a Levite (Acts 4:36). Given that fact, and the confidence invested in Barnabas by the church in Jerusalem when an issue of purity arose (Acts 11:22), it is natural to infer that Barnabas was discreet in his social contacts with non-Jewish believers. Even Paul does not say of Barnabas, as he does of Peter, that he ate commonly with non-Jews and then separated when emissaries from James arrived (see Gal. 2:11–13). Barnabas's policy was probably consistent and accepted non-Jews in baptism, although they continued to be treated as non-Jews after baptism.

Barnabas represents a committed attempt to convert Peter's dual loyalty — to the spirit in baptism and to circumcision and purity within Israel — into a coherent social policy. Paul calls the attempt hypocritical because he did not agree with it; in fact it was a brilliant effort to combine inclusiveness with integrity. Acts attempts to minimize the difference between Barnabas and Paul, turning it into a limited matter of who should accompany them in a visit to churches they had preached to previously (see Acts 15:36–41). In fact, their dispute after the Apostolic Council turned around what had always divided them: Barnabas's commitment to separate fellowship in order to preserve the purity of Israel. The person Barnabas wanted to come with them, John called Mark, had been associated with the circle of Peter and was well received in Jerusalem (see Acts 12:12–17, 25; 13:5, 15). (Paul no doubt feared that John Mark would further ex-

tend the influence of James.) Barnabas stood by the policy that
fellowship among non-Jewish Christians was authorized and
endorsed but that the separate fellowship of Israel was also to
be maintained.

The social policy of the community as envisaged by Barnabas
is instanced in the two stories of feeding, of the five thousand
and the four thousand. Both stories reflect a eucharistic fellowship with Jesus, one for Israel and one for non-Jews. That
crucial meaning is the key to what has long perplexed commentators, the significance of the numerological symbols that
are embedded in each story and that function in contrast to one
another.

In the first story (Matt. 14:13–21; Mark 6:32–44; Luke 9:10b–
17), the eucharistic associations are plain:[6] Jesus blesses and
breaks the bread prior to distribution (Matt. 14:19; Mark 6:41;
Luke 9:16). That emphasis so consumes the story that the fish —
characteristic among Christian eucharistic symbols[7] — are of
subsidiary significance by the end of the passage (cf. Mark 6:43
with Matt. 14:20 and Luke 9:17). Whatever the pericope represented originally, it becomes a eucharistic narrative in the
Barnaban presentation. Jesus gathers people in an orderly way
(see Matt. 14:18; Mark 6:39, 40; Luke 9:14, 15), by "symposia"
as Mark literally has it (6:39); without that order, they might be
described as sheep without a shepherd (Mark 6:34).

The *Didache* (9:4) relates the prayer that just as bread is scattered on the mountains (in the form of wheat)[8] and yet may
be gathered into one, so the Church might be gathered into

---

6. See Alan Hugh McNeile, *The Gospel according to St. Matthew* (London:
Macmillan, 1957), 216, and C. E. B. Cranfield, *The Gospel according to St Mark*,
Cambridge Greek Testament Commentary (Cambridge: Cambridge University Press, 1963), 222, 223. Cranfield also notes the associations between the
feeding stories, eucharistic celebration, and the motif of the manna in the
wilderness. Moreover, he picks up the sense of *sumposia sumposia* in Mark 6:39
(p. 218). See also W. D. Davies and Dale C. Allison, *A Critical and Exegetical Commentary on the Gospel according to Saint Matthew*, International Critical
Commentary (Edinburgh: T. and T. Clark, 1991), 2:481, 493, 494.

7. See C. H. Dodd, *Historical Tradition in the Fourth Gospel* (Cambridge:
Cambridge University Press, 1965), 200, 201. Davies and Allison (*Critical and
Exegetical Commentary*, 481) refer to 2 Bar. 29:3–8 and 4 Ezra 6:52 to support their suggestion that "both bread (or manna) and fish (or Leviathan) are
associated with the messianic feast in many Jewish texts."

8. Charles Taylor cited Ps. 72:16 in order to instance the imagery of

the Father's kingdom. The five thousand congregate in such a manner, their very number a multiple of the prophetic gathering in 2 Kings 4:42–44. There, Elisha feeds one hundred men with twenty loaves of barley, so that the multitude in Mark 6 (and its Synoptic parallels) has been increased by factors of ten and five. The number ten is of symbolic significance within the biblical tradition, most famously in the case of the ten "words" or commandments of Exod. 34:28.[9] The number five, one-fourth the number of loaves in the story about Elisha, also corresponds to the Pythagorean number of man, in that the outline of four limbs and a head approximate a pentagram.[10]

The authority of the Twelve is a marked concern within the story. Their return in Matt. 14:12b, 13; Mark 6:30, 31; Luke 9:10a after their commission (see Matt. 10:1–42; Mark 6:7–13; Luke 9:1–6) is what occasions the feeding, and their function in the proceedings is definite: Jesus gives them the bread, to give it to others (Matt. 14:19; Mark 6:41; Luke 9:16). Their place here is cognate with their position within another pericope (from the Jacobean cycle) that features the Twelve: the parable of the sower, its interpretation, and the assertion that only the Twelve possess the mystery of the kingdom (Matt. 13:1–17; Mark 4:1–12; Luke 8:4–10).[11] Such a mystery is also conveyed here, in the assertion that twelve baskets of fragments were gathered after the five thousand ate. The lesson is evident: the Twelve, the counterparts of the twelve tribes of Israel, will always have enough to feed the Church, which is understood to realize the identity of Israel in the wilderness.[12]

The story of the feeding of the four thousand (Matt. 15:32–39; Mark 8:1–10) follows so exactly that of the five thousand that its omission by Luke may seem understandable, simply

---

grain growing on mountains (*The Teaching of the Twelve Apostles* [Cambridge: Deighton Bell, 1886], 129, 130).

9. Jöram Friberg, "Numbers and Counting," in *Anchor Bible Dictionary,* ed. D. N. Freedman (New York: Doubleday, 1992), 1145.

10. See Annemarie Schimmel, "Numbers: An Overview," in *The Encyclopedia of Religion,* ed. M. Eliade (New York: Macmillan, 1987), 13–19.

11. See Bruce D. Chilton, *A Galilean Rabbi and His Bible* (Wilmington, Del.: Glazier, 1984), 95, 96.

12. The implicit association with Israel in the wilderness, feeding on manna, is developed in John 6.

as a redundant doublet. But there are distinctive elements in the second feeding story. Four thousand is a multiple of the four points of the compass; further, the story follows that of the Canaanite or Syrophoenician woman (Matt. 15:21–28; Mark 7:24–30) and concerns a throng from a number of different areas and backgrounds (see Matt. 15:21, 29; Mark 7:24, 31). The issue of non-Jewish contact with Jesus is therefore marked here, in a way it is not in the case of the feeding of the five thousand. Likewise, the number seven, the number of bushels of fragments here collected, corresponds to the deacons of the Hellenists in the church of Jerusalem (see Acts 6:1–6) and is related to the traditional number of the seventy nations within Judaism.[13]

Moreover, the reference to Jesus as giving thanks (*eukharistesas*) over the bread in Matt. 15:36 and Mark 8:6 better corresponds to the Hellenistic version of the Petrine eucharist in Luke 22:17, 19 and 1 Cor. 11:24 than does "he blessed" (*eulogesen*) in Matt. 14:19 and Mark 6:39, which better corresponds to the earlier Petrine formula of eucharist in Matt. 26:26 and Mark 14:22.[14]

The Lukan omission of such stories, in fact of the whole of what corresponds to Mark 6:45–8:26 (conventionally designated as "the great omission" of Mark by Luke), seems natural, once their meaning is appreciated: they concern the sense of Jesus in an environment characterized by a mixture of Jews and Gentiles.[15] Luke takes up that theme in Acts and regards its reversion into the ministry of Jesus as an anachronism.

After the second feeding, Jesus rebukes his disciples for a failure to understand when he warns them about the leaven of the Pharisees and others and asks whether they truly grasp the

---

13. See Friberg, "Numbers and Counting," 1145.

14. See Davies and Allison (*Critical and Exegetical Commentary,* 562–65) for a discussion of the features here adduced. Their conclusion that the story does not concern only Gentiles, but (in the Matthean formulation) "the lost sheep of the house of Israel" (p. 564), seems justified. Nonetheless, the geographical references that precede the second feeding make it apparent that the four thousand were not simply Jews in a conventionally recognizable sense.

15. That the feeding of the four thousand relates particularly to Gentiles is argued, for example, in John W. Bowman, *The Gospel of Mark: The New Christian Passover Haggadah,* Studia Postbiblica (Leiden: Brill, 1965), 176–78.

relationship between the number twelve and the five thousand and the number seven and the four thousand (Matt. 16:5–12; Mark 8:14–21). In the mind of the Hellenistic catechesis, the meaning is clear, and its implications for eucharistic discipline are evident.[16] Celebration of eucharist in its truest sense is neither to be limited to Jews, as the Jacobean program would have it, nor forced upon communities in a way that would require Jews to accept reduced standards of purity, as the Pauline program would have it. The Hellenistic catechesis of which the Synoptic transformation is a monument provides for an ongoing apostolate for Jews (the Twelve) and Gentiles (the Seven), prepared to feed as many of the Church that gather.[17]

For all the careful power of the Barnaban symbolism within the stories of the five thousand and the four thousand, a largely inadvertent development of meaning was even more widely influential. When Jesus distributed bread during the course of his last meals in Jerusalem, he referred to it as his "flesh." He meant that his fellowship in meals took over from the practice of sacrifice in the Temple, as we have discussed in volume 1 (chap. 5). Similarly, the celebratory wine took over the function of blood. But by 50 C.E., when the Barnaban catechesis emerged within an elaborate narrative of Jesus' passion, a shift in meaning had occurred.

From the time that the narrative of the passion provided the governing context of Jesus' words during his eucharistic celebrations, the bread and the wine were related to Jesus' body and blood in a personal sense. The constant focus on Jesus' own fate within the passion narrative made that development inevitable. The flesh and blood of sacrifice were transformed into means of solidarity with the noble martyr. That transformation was not merely a function of the linguistic decision to render "flesh" (*bisra'*) in Aramaic with "body" (*soma*) in Greek, although that decision fed a deeper, cultural process of trans-

---

16. See Paul J. Achtemeier (*Mark*, Proclamation Commentaries [Philadelphia: Fortress, 1986], 29), who rightly observes that the statement attributed to Jesus "presupposes not only the present order of events in Mark, but also the present form of the Greek prose." His conclusion of particularly Markan authorship, however, is not warranted.

17. For further discussion, see Chilton, *Feast of Meanings*, 93–130.

formation. There was no possibility of preventing at least some Hellenistic Christians who followed the eucharistic practice of the Synoptics from conceiving of Jesus himself as consumed in the bread and wine.

Jesus' last supper was naturally compared to initiation into Mystery within Hellenistic Christianity. Jesus was a new Dionysus, historical rather than mythical, who gave himself, flesh and blood, in the meals that were held in his name. After all, he had said "This is my body," and "This is my blood." For many Hellenistic Christians, that could only mean that Jesus referred to himself: bread and wine were tokens of Jesus, which became his body and blood when believers consumed them.[18]

The Johannine discourse concerning the bread of life, following upon a paschal reading of the feeding of the five thousand, addressed the challenges of a Hellenistic understanding of eucharist as Mystery. By means of a nuanced tension between "flesh" in its ordinary sense (6:63), as alien from God, and Jesus' "flesh" as the medium through which the son of man was sent by God to offer life (6:53–59), the Johannine discourse avoided any crude reduction of eucharist to the consumption of a god. Jesus' flesh is that bread that he gives (6:51), the true manna, a miracle that animates the world (6:32, 33), because he is himself the bread of life (6:35, 48, 51). The essential nuance, apart from which the discourse is not understandable, is that Jesus' "flesh" as consumed in eucharist is not flesh in the usual understanding but the means by which he offers spirit and life (6:63). Yet however sophisticated the discourse may be, it implicitly accepts that the language of Mystery is appropriate, suitably refined, for the description of eucharist. For that reason, the Fourth Gospel marks the point at which the Christian practice of eucharist self-consciously and definitively parted from Judaism, even as the imagery of exodus and Passover was embraced and developed.

John's theology held that personal solidarity with Jesus was effected in eucharistic practice. That overarching meaning could

---

18. See Samuel Angus, *The Mystery-Religions and Christianity: A Study in the Religious Background of Early Christianity* (London: Murray, 1925), 127–33; Kurt Rudolf, "Mystery Religions," in *The Encyclopedia of Religion*, ed. M. Eliade, trans. M. J. O'Connell (New York: Macmillan 1987), 10:230–39.

be developed because the Barnaban cycle had already associated Jesus' "body" and "blood" with the passion and had established the eucharistic meanings of the feeding stories. But unlike John, the Barnaban cycle held to the integrity of Israel as well as the inclusion of non-Jews. John presents no analogue of the feeding of the four thousand because the scope of the feeding of the five thousand is already held to include "all that the Father gives me" (6:37). Moreover, John places Philip within the episode (6:5, 7), and Philip is understood to be Jesus' contact with "Greeks" (so John 12:20–50).

Contrast with the Johannine presentation of the eucharistic feeding of the five thousand makes the Barnaban framing of both feeding stories all the more striking. The twelve baskets are available for Israel; the seven baskets are available for non-Jews who are baptized. Both groups, each belonging to the Church of all those who are called out by God and who accept bearing the name of Christ, enjoy solidarity with Christ himself by partaking of his body and blood. The body of Christ had become an identity that all could share within the Church, whatever else might divide them.

Paul's Development of "the Body of Christ"

As a consequence of his association with Barnabas in the leadership of Hellenistic congregations (Antioch preeminently), Paul was well familiar with the eucharistic meaning of the phrase "the body of Christ." As John A. T. Robinson pointed out in a study that remains valuable, "The words of institution of the Last Supper, 'This is my body,' contain the only instance of a quasi-theological use of the word which is certainly pre-Pauline."[19]

For Paul, eucharist involved an active recollection of the passion: "For as many times as you eat this bread and drink the cup, you announce the Lord's death, until he comes" (1 Cor. 11:26). Paul repeats a key term of reference within the eucharistic tradition in his own voice and draws his conclusion

---

19. John A. T. Robinson, *The Body: A Study in Pauline Theology*, Studies in Biblical Theology 5 (London: SCM, 1961), 56.

(*gar* [for]), which is that the significance of the eucharist is
to be found in the death of Jesus. Eucharistic fellowship de-
clares that Jesus died and — at the same time — awaits his
parousia.

Paul's assumption is that Jesus' last meal, the paradigm of
the Lord's Supper, was of covenantal significance, a sacrificial "memorial" that was associated with the death of Jesus in
particular. His wording, which refers to Jesus' cup as a new covenant in his blood (1 Cor. 11:25), agrees with the later version of
Petrine tradition that is reflected in Luke (22:20), the Synoptic
Gospel that has the strongest associations with Antioch.[20] It is
likely that Paul's version of the Petrine tradition derived from
his period in Antioch, his primary base by his own testimony
(in Galatians 2) until his break with Barnabas.

Paul's development of the concept of "the body of Christ"
was just that: a development, rather than an original contribution. His commitment to the traditional theology was fierce, as
he goes on in 1 Corinthians to indicate:

> So whoever eats the bread and drinks the cup of the Lord
> unworthily will be answerable to the body and blood of
> the Lord. Let a man examine himself, and then eat from
> the bread and drink from the cup. For one who eats and
> drinks without discerning the body, eats and drinks judg-
> ment against himself. For this reason, many are weak and
> ill among you, and quite a number have died. (11:27–30)

Paul's last statement, which associates disease with unworthy
participation in eucharist, shows how near the symbolic association of the bread and wine with Jesus' body and blood came to
being a claim for the miraculous power of that food.

Long before the Johannine comparison of Jesus' flesh with
the manna God gave his people in the wilderness, Paul had
arrived at the same thought. The analogy is developed in the
material immediately preceding Paul's presentation of eucharistic tradition (1 Corinthians 10). Christ himself is presented as
the typological meaning of Passover, as the entire complex of
the exodus — including crossing the sea and eating miraculous

---

20. The wordings of Matt. 26:28 and of Mark 14:24 are quite different.

food (Exodus 13–17) — is presented as "types" in 1 Cor. 10:6. The cloud that led Israel and the sea they crossed correspond to baptism (vv. 1, 2), while the food they ate and the water provided from the rock correspond to eucharist (vv. 3–4).[21] Typology also enables Paul to make the connection between the idolatry in the wilderness and the fornication in Corinth, which is one of his preoccupations (vv. 6–14), but the initial correspondence, between exodus and both baptism and eucharist, is essential to his argument, and he labors the point with the introduction, "I would not have you ignorant, brethren..." (v. 1).

Within the order of exposition Paul follows, the imagery begins with the cloud and the sea, proceeds through the food in the wilderness, and ends with the water from the rock; the correspondence is to the water (and spirit) of baptism, the bread of eucharist, and the wine of eucharist, respectively (1 Cor. 10:1–4). The typological key to the sequence is provided by the Pauline exposition of the rock from which drink flowed: "And the rock was Christ" (10:4).[22] Paul demonstrates how, in the setting of Hellenistic Christianity, a paschal reading of the eucharist was an important element within a typology of Jesus himself as Passover.

It has frequently been objected that the eucharistic meaning of "the body of Christ" does not explain Paul's usage overall because the concept of eating the body is quite different from being the body.[23] But the transition from the eucharistic meaning of the phrase to the corporate meaning of the phrase is not strained, as Paul himself indicates:

> The cup of blessing which we bless, is it not fellowship in the blood of Christ? The bread which we break, is it not fellowship in the body of Christ? Because there is one

---

21. For a useful exposition, see Gordon D. Fee, *The First Epistle to the Corinthians*, New International Commentary (Grand Rapids: Eerdmans, 1987), 443–50.

22. See Oscar Cullmann, "πέτρα," in *Theological Dictionary of the New Testament*, ed. G. Friedrich, trans. G. W Bromiley (Grand Rapids: Eerdmans, 1979), 16:95–99, 97.

23. See R. Y. K. Fung, "Body of Christ," in *Dictionary of Paul and His Letters*, 77.

bread, we are one body, although we are many, because we all share from the one bread. (1 Cor. 10:16–17)

Paul goes on in his letters to develop that insight in many ways, and later writings in his name were to articulate the motif even further. But in the passage just cited, Paul shows us both the origin and the direction of his understanding of "the body of Christ." It begins with the Hellenistic theology of eucharist, in which consuming the bread identifies the believer with Christ's death, and it consummates in the declaration that all who share that bread are incorporated into Christ, as into a single body.

The transition is natural for Paul because he was familiar with the Hellenistic conception of corporate "body," which was especially popularized by Stoic writers. The evidence is neatly summarized by Jürgen Becker:

Agrippa M. Lanatus, for example, exhorted the plebeians not to break off fellowship with the city of Rome because, as in a human organism, all members need each other (Livy, *Ab urbe condita* 2.32–33). Plato also compares the state with an organism and, as in 1 Cor. 12:26, emphasizes the suffering and rejoicing of the members together (Plato, *Republic* 462C-D). Seneca can see the state as the body of the emperor, who is the soul of the body (Seneca, *De clementia* 1.5.1).[24]

Becker claims that Paul "was probably the first to transfer this idea to a religious communion," but that is an incautious generalization. Philo, after all, observes that the high priest's sacrifice welds Israel together "into one and the same family as though it were a single body" (Philo, *De specialibus legibus* 3.131).

Becker is on firmer ground in his observation that, for Paul, "the body of Christ" is no mere metaphor but describes the living solidarity of those who share the spirit of God by means of baptism and eucharist.[25] Again, Paul is the best commentator on his own thought. In 1 Corinthians 12, just after he has

---

24. Jürgen Becker, *Paul: Apostle to the Gentiles*, trans. O. C. Dean (Louisville: Westminster/John Knox, 1993), 428.

25. Even here, however, there is a continuing dispute; see Fung, "Body of Christ," 78, where it is concluded that one *should* view "the body concept

discussed the eucharist, he explains in a fairly predictable way how diverse members belong to a single body. In the midst of that discussion, he puts forward the "body of Christ" as the principal definition of the Church:

> For just as the body is one and has many members, and all the members of the body (being many) are one body, so is Christ. For in one spirit we were all baptized into one body — whether Jews or Greeks, slave or free — and we all were given to drink of one spirit. (1 Cor. 12:12–13)

By focusing on the "body" as the medium of eucharistic solidarity and then developing its corporate meaning, Paul turns the traditional, Petrine understanding of spirit (as received in baptism) into the *single* principle of Christian identity. His reply to any attempt to form discrete fellowships within the Church will now always be, "Is Christ divided?" (so 1 Cor. 1:13).

The further articulation of "the body of Christ" by Paul and his successors is easily traced. As in the case of 1 Corinthians 12 (and, by way of anticipation, 1 Cor. 6:15), the point in Rom. 12:4–8 is that the society of those who are joined in Christ's body is itself a body that finds its unity in diversity and its diversity in unity. Two deutero-Pauline letters, Colossians and Ephesians, shift the application of the image of the body. Because the identification of the Church with Christ's body is taken as read in Colossians (see Col. 1:18, 24), Christ himself is portrayed as the head of that body (Col. 1:18; 2:19), in order to stress his preeminence. That portrayal is pursued in Ephesians (1:22–23; 4:15–16), to the point that Christ as "head" of the Church can be thought of as distinct from her, along the lines of a husband from a wife (Eph. 5:21–33).

The startling quality of the Pauline conception of "the body of Christ" does not derive from how it is developed within the letters written by Paul or later attributed to Paul. That trajectory is a relatively consistent product of the interaction between the eucharistic theology of solidarity with Christ, which was common within Hellenistic Christianity, and the quasi-Stoic

---

metaphorically, not literally and biologically or mystically." I take it that such contentions tell us more about the continuing inheritance of the Reformation than about Paul, so that the issue may be left for another occasion.

language of incorporation into a single body that Paul himself had learned in Tarsus, his home.[26] The radical feature of Pauline usage is to be found not in the development of the concept but in the claim that the Church is defined *solely* in respect of this "body." Whether Jew or Greek, only incorporation into Christ mattered to Paul (so 1 Cor. 12:12–13). The consequence of that univocal definition is spelled out in Ephesians (after the motif of the body has been invoked): the dividing line between Jews and non-Jews had been set aside definitively in Christ (Eph. 2:11–22).

Paul's understanding of the body of Christ comports well with his definition of Israel (a topic that took up our attention in volume 1 [chap. 4]). Just as he argued in Galatians that to believe in Christ was to fulfill the faith of Abraham, so he argued in 1 Corinthians that such faith made believers one body in Christ. The idiom of Galatians, written around 53 C.E., is biblical; that of 1 Corinthians, written around 56 C.E., is philosophical. But both letters in their differing ways implicitly raise the question of Israel. If belief fulfills the vocation of Abraham and incorporates the believer into Christ, what further value can be attached to what the Scriptures call Israel? That is a question that Paul himself addresses at length in his letter to the Romans.

Paul is never more himself than in Romans chapters 9–11, which is just where he frames the issue of Israel in a way that became classic for Christianity. Romans itself is the most mature of the genuinely Pauline letters, written to a community that Paul had not personally founded. His letter to the Romans is, in effect, a fulsome introduction to his own thinking, and the main lines of Paul's argument seem reasonably clear. But the form of his argumentation, with its many references to Scripture and deductions from Scripture, strikes most readers as both foreign and convoluted. Why is a basically simple idea wrapped up in an esoteric package? As we shall see, that question will itself require refinement as we encounter Paul's thinking, but it will serve us well as we first approach our text.

An observant student could sketch out a précis of Paul's

---

26. In regard to the cultural milieu of Tarsus, see Becker, *Paul*, 35–36.

thought in Romans 9–11 *without* reference to the Scripture he cites. The result would be a reasonable, self-contained address, which could be delivered succinctly:

> Although I am distressed that my people have not accepted the gospel (9:1–5), their failure is not God's: it is just that he has, as always, chosen freely whom he wills (9:6–13). That might seem hard, but God is sovereign in the matter of choice (9:14–23), and he has simply decided to call both Jews and Gentiles (9:24–33).[27]
>
> There is now no distinction between Jew and Greek in the matter of salvation: if you confess the Lord Jesus and believe God raised him from the dead, you will be saved (10:1–21, v. 9). Those who are believers must not, however, imagine that God has rejected his people. After all, there are some Jews who do believe in Jesus (11:1–10), and even those who do not believe have, in their lack of faith, provided an opportunity for Gentiles (11:11–24). Once the fullness of the Gentiles is accomplished, all Israel, including both Jews and Gentiles, will be seen to be saved (11:25–36).

There are, of course, crucial facets within each of the statements in the above précis that remain to be explored, but they are subsidiary to the main lines of the argument. What becomes unmistakably clear, when we boil Paul's ornate speech down to its essentials, is that he is making a cogent case for a particular view of how God's saving activity in Christ Jesus is consistent with his election of Israel. Once it is clear that Israel is *elected*, not sovereign, so that divine choice is operative, rather than divine right, Paul's observations follow logically.

Paul's design at this point comports well with the purpose of his letter to the Romans as a whole and makes sense within the Hellenistic environment in which he functioned. Stanley Stowers has explained that the writing of letters, whether at the common level of incidental discourse or with a refined standard

---

27. A break at 9:24 is more plausible in Greek than in English; see the twenty-sixth edition of *Novum Testamentum Graece*, eds. E. Nestle and K. Aland (Stuttgart: Deutsche Bibelstiftung, 1979).

of rhetoric, was conventional within the culture of the Mediterranean Basin and is a natural context in which to understand much of the New Testament.[28] That convention also influenced ancient Judaism, which — despite the impression of an isolated phenomenon that some writers give — was itself a lively constituent within the cultural life of its time.[29] But Stowers is well within the scholarly consensus when he concludes that Judaism did not actively appropriate the convention and transmit it directly to Christianity.[30]

Specifically, Paul in Romans appears to be writing a "protreptic letter," by which Stowers means a work designed to convert the reader to Paul's set of teachings. Stowers is able on the basis of a comparison with Graeco-Roman convention to argue that the entire letter is designed to present Paul's gospel of salvation for Gentiles and to defend it against the charge that it means the loss of Israel's salvation.[31] The analysis of Romans according to its function within its most plausible social setting therefore helps us to identify the main lines of its purpose.

Indeed, the clarity of function that emerges from such an approach may appear to be at odds with the convoluted character of Paul's argument. Even if Romans is a "protreptic letter,"

---

28. Stanley Stowers, *Letter Writing in Greco-Roman Antiquity*, Library of Early Christianity (Philadelphia: Westminster, 1986), 25.

29. Ibid., 41–42. Within the Hebrew Bible, Stowers cites 2 Sam. 11:14, 15; 1 Kings 21:8–10; 2 Kings 10:1–6; 19:9–14; Ezra 4–5. The last two passages, of course, relate Assyrian and Persian letters (and the second should be extended to 6:12). Moreover, all of the passages cited concern royal, official, or military communication, rather than the sort of cultural activity that is reflected in the New Testament. Stowers's references to Philo, Josephus, and 1 and 2 Maccabees are more on target.

30. Stowers (*Letter Writing*) does not, however, make reference to the letters of Bar Kokhba and to the evidence of correspondence between Antioch and Palestine; both sorts of letter are of direct pertinence to his theme. See J. A. Fitzmyer, "Aramaic Epistolography," in *Wandering Aramean: Collected Aramaic Essays*, SBL Monograph Series 25 (Chico, Calif.: Scholars Press, 1979), 183–204; W. A. Meeks and R. L. Wilken, *Jews and Christians in Antioch in the First Four Centuries of the Common Era*, SBL Sources for Biblical Study 13 (Ann Arbor: Scholars Press, 1978).

31. Stowers, *Letter Writing*, 113, 114. See also M. L. Stirewalt, "Appendix: The Form and Function of the Greek Letter-Essay," in *The Romans Debate*, ed. K. P. Donfried (Minneapolis: Augsburg, 1977), 175–206, and Donfried, "False Presuppositions in the Study of Romans," in *The Romans Debate*, 120–48.

the involved argument from Scripture in chapters 9–11 is obviously the result of a dynamic not evidenced by the letter as a whole. Of course, Scripture does play a crucial role in Romans generally (as it does normally in Pauline thought), but the consistency of recourse to textual argument makes our chapters appear distinctive.[32]

Before we consider why Paul's form of argumentation in Romans 9–11 is exegetical in a way most of the letter is not, we must first appreciate how the simple, discursive case Paul makes is enhanced by means of reference to Scripture. At each major point in the argument, well-known passages of Scripture are cited.

A crucial bridge is provided by narratives concerning Isaac. In Rom. 9:7, Paul quotes Gen. 21:12, "After Isaac shall your seed be named." Now that reference may appear simply to be an instance of using a "proof-text," chosen pretty much at random from a much larger number of those that might have been cited. But the quotation comes at the climax of a story in which God tells Abraham to accede to Sarah's demand and cast out Hagar and Ishmael, "for the son of this slave woman shall not inherit with my son Isaac" (Gen. 21:10).

The analogy with the situation Paul believes he addresses is striking. He spells the analogy out in Rom. 9:8, "That is, these children of flesh are not children of God, but children of the promise are reckoned as the seed." Of course, that finding requires that Isaac correspond to the promise, and Paul makes out just that correspondence. In Rom. 9:9, he quotes Gen. 18:14 (or perhaps v. 10), "At this time (next year) I will come, and Sarah will have a son." That verse, of course, is resonant since it caps the story of God's visitation at Mamre: Sarah laughs (v. 12) and is blessed with Isaac, whose name means "he laughs," because it is God's joke in the end. In Paul's argument, the apparent frivolity of God's sovereign choice is a serious principle, attested in Scripture.

The pattern established in Rom. 9:6–9 is followed consistently in the chapters we are concerned with. At first, Paul does

---

32. See R. Badenas, *Christ the End of the Law: Rom. 10:4 in Pauline Perspective,* Journal for the Study of the New Testament Supplement Series 10 (Sheffield, Eng.: JSOT, 1985), 90–92.

not cite a specific Scripture in what follows, but he does invoke the general case of Rebecca and Isaac (9:10, 11). She conceived twins, and before they did anything, or were even born, Rebecca was told, "The greater will serve the lesser" (Rom. 9:12; Gen. 25:23). At issue, of course, is the rivalry between Esau and Jacob, which is a major motif of Genesis. Paul sums it all up with a quotation from Malachi, "I loved Jacob and hated Esau" (Rom. 9:13; Mal. 1:2, 3). That Paul can draw upon Malachi's appropriation of the motif in Genesis is especially compelling: he implicitly claims that his analogy has prophetic warrant. The fundamentals of his scriptural reasoning are drawn from the Torah, but the nature of his reasoning, he claims, is in line with that of the prophets.

Paul appears to have operated within the conventional categorization of the Hebrew Bible in Judaism. That categorization recognized divisions of the canon into the Torah (the Pentateuch), the Prophets (including the Former Prophets, from Joshua through 2 Kings, and the Latter Prophets, more familiarly considered prophetic in English), and the Writings (an essentially miscellaneous category). Paul simply assumes the coherence and consistency of the canon.

It is indicative of the consistency of Pauline rhetoric that he now moves from Genesis to Exodus. That shift in scriptural foundation, at 9:14–15, corresponds precisely to the development of Paul's argument (see the précis above): having rejoiced in God's sovereign choice as the fulfillment of promise, Paul now defends God's sovereignty against the charge that it is unjust or arbitrary (9:14). God said to Moses, "I will have mercy on whom I have mercy, and I will show compassion to whom I will show compassion" (Exod. 33:19; Rom. 9:15). In Exodus, God speaks of his mercy and compassion just as he is revealing his goodness to Moses; Paul's point is that God's choices are consistent with his just revelation to Moses.

In the statement to Moses in Exod. 33:19, the narrative setting connects the definition of God's people with his revelation of his name and glory (Exod. 33:12–23): what is at issue is the very nature of God and nature of his people together. A particular case in Exodus of God deciding not to have mercy, as Paul says (9:18), is that of Pharaoh, of whom Scripture says, "For this purpose I have raised you up, that I might display my power over you, and that my name might be announced in all the earth" (Rom. 9:17; Exod. 9:16).[33] God's "name" is at issue in both passages in Exodus that have been cited (33:19 and 9:16), and their association betrays Paul's almost midrashic logic (see below), in which Scripture is held in different places and contexts to address the same issues coherently.

The assumption of that coherence is carried over to the prophets: Isaiah (29:16; 45:9, in Rom. 9:20) and Jeremiah (18:6, in Rom. 9:21) are used to demonstrate that it is misguided for a vessel of punishment to answer back to its maker. Consideration of Isa. 29:16, 45:9 and Jer. 18:6 within their literary contexts shows that Paul is still attending carefully to the sense of the passages he cites. In all, the paramount issue is the fate of Israel, as determined by a sovereign God.

The next development of Paul's argument, at 9:24–25 (again, see the précis), again corresponds to a shift in canonical focus. By citing Hosea and Isaiah, Paul demonstrates that we who are called by God are from both Jews and Gentiles (9:24). First, Hosea shows — at least, to Paul's satisfaction — that Gentiles are to be included among God's people (9:25, 26). Paul garbles the quotation from Hosea, drawing first from 2:23 and then from 1:10, and here is stretching to make a point. Hosea is contextually concerned with the restoration of Israel, not the inclusion of Gentiles; Paul reads what he takes to be a general truth of Scripture into a passage in which that meaning has no literary place.

He returns to his usual, more acute interpretation in 9:27–29 when he cites passages from Isaiah by way of arguing that Jews as such are not chosen, but that a remnant from their ranks is to be saved (Isa. 10:22; 28:22; and Isa. 1:9). But he cites a curious and creative mixture of Isa. 28:16 and 8:14 in Rom. 9:33, in order to show that the principle of selecting from the elect places a

---

33. Generally, Paul's text is practically identical with the emerging text of the Septuagint, but he may have been influenced occasionally (as here) by Targumic interpretations and by the original Hebrew (see Bruce D. Chilton, *God in Strength: Jesus' Announcement of the Kingdom:* The Biblical Seminar [Sheffield, England: JSOT, 1987], 267, 273, 274).

stone of stumbling and a rock of offense in the midst of Israel (Rom. 9:30–32).

Paul's exegetical method is never more complex than in Romans 9, and we need to pause for breath before proceeding further. Although the details of the Pauline execution may dazzle us (as they were no doubt intended to), the fact is that certain characteristic traits are plain. Paul argues from the Torah that (1) God operates by fulfilling promises (9:1–13), and that (2) those promises are kept for those chosen by God (9:14–23). He then purports to demonstrate from the Prophets that God has chosen his people from among Jews and Gentiles (9:24–33). On the whole, but for two exceptions, Paul cites his passages with care and contextual sensitivity, which means that any reader will better appreciate the argument if he or she is familiar with the Scriptures of Israel.

The two exceptions to Paul's care and sensitivity are instructive. As we have seen, he reads Gentiles into Hosea (9:25, 26) and splices together two verses of Isaiah (9:33). These are not mere lapses on Paul's part. To his mind, the entry of Gentiles among the ranks of God's chosen and the coming of Christ as a rock of offense to many in Israel are facts of experience that coexist with and interpret facts of Scripture. Paul's "text" is not merely Scripture but his awareness, and others' awareness, that Jesus is God's son.[34]

Once these interpretative characteristics of Paul's argument are appreciated, Romans 10 and 11 may more briefly be summarized from the point of view of their reference to Scripture. In chapter 10, Paul makes his famous, daring assertion that, in Deut. 30:11–14, when Moses refers to the nearness of the commandment, he means not any precise instruction but the presence of Christ, who can be neither brought down from heaven nor brought up from the abyss, except by God's sure command (Rom. 10:6–8).

How does Paul know the Scriptures, properly understood, adduce Christ? He has just told us in Rom. 10:4, "Christ is

---

34. Comparison may be invited with the approach of Jesus to Scripture, in which the kingdom is held to be the hermeneutical center of the Scriptures (see Chilton, *Galilean Rabbi*). For Paul, Christ is that center (see Rom. 10:4).

the point of the law, for the righteousness of every believer."[35] By again citing Isa. 28:16, in verse 11, Paul may betray his own awareness that he is invoking Christ, rather than deducing Christ, at this point. The other usages in chapter 10 — of Lev. 18:5[36] in 10:5, of Joel 3:5 in 10:13, of Isa. 52:7 in 10:15, of Isa. 53:1 in 10:16, of Ps. 19:4[37] in 10:18, and of Isa. 65:1, 2 in 10:20, 21 — fall within the more usual Pauline range of texts that illustrate a coherent principle.

Chapter 11 may be surveyed even more summarily because the usages of Scripture are all illustrative. There are no special invocations of Christ or of the motif of the inclusion of the Gentiles. Until this point, the bulk of Paul's references have come from the Torah and the Latter Prophets. Now he brings balance to his case scripturally by citing the instance of Elijah from the Former Prophets. Again, attention to the contexts of the Scriptures Paul cites richly rewards itself. The assertion that God has not rejected his people in 11:2, drawn from 1 Sam. 12:22, comes in a context in which the prophet Samuel assures Israel that, despite their wickedness, God's choice is constant (1 Sam. 12:19–25). The close of that passage, however, does threaten, "But if you act wickedly, you shall be swept away, both you and your king" (1 Sam. 12:25). Wickedness does not revoke God's choice, but it does alter its scope.

In other words, the thought of the remnant, which has been an explicit part of the argument since 9:27, 28 (by means of the citation of Isa. 10:22, 23), has remained with Paul throughout. For that reason, the reference to Elijah in 11:2b–5 (see 1 Kings 19:1–18, and vv. 10, 14, and 18 in particular) is apposite: there is a prophetic analogy for the circumstances Paul finds himself in, where only a radical minority has kept faith. Once it is established that the residue of the remnant can be deliberately hardened in their rebellion (see Deut. 29:3[38] in 11:8 and

---

35. See Badenas, *Christ*, 144–55. Badenas himself does not render τέλος as "point," but such a rendering would be consistent with his case.

36. Notably, this command, in its context, requires separation from the Gentiles, which supports the understanding that, as in Gal. 3:12, Paul cites the passage in order to overturn it with a principle of inclusion.

37. Psalm 18:5 in the Septuagint and 19:5 in the Masoretic Text.

38. With reverberations with Isa. 6:9, 10; 29:10.

Ps. 69:22, 23[39] in 11:9), there is no further need of scriptural warrant for what Paul argues.

He does, however, offer a final citation of Isaiah (59:20, 21 and 27:9) in 11:26, 27, by way of making his comprehensive assertion that "all Israel" — but a chastened, forgiven Israel, not a claimant as of right — is to be saved.[40] At this crucial moment, he must again splice Scriptures, not merely cite them, to achieve the dual stress on deliverance and forgiveness that is the apogee of his argument.

We may set out mentally, as it were side by side, two analyses of Romans 9–11. Followed along one track, the chapters instance protreptic discourse, in which Paul appeals to his readers to follow his way of thinking. He wishes to convince them that God's inclusion of believing Gentiles with Jews who accept Jesus as Christ represents a fulfillment of the promise to Israel. Followed along the second track, the same chapters represent a carefully orchestrated argument from all the main sections of the Hebrew canon, cited in translation, which is designed to sweep readers up in the promise that all Israel — forgiven Jews and Gentiles — is to be saved (11:26, 27).

It is obvious that the two tracks of analysis are complementary, and neither alone would adequately account for the chapters as a whole. But it is equally obvious that the chapters are crafted as a whole: the references to Scripture not only are keyed to major developments of the argument but contribute those developments. It is not a matter of discursive thought merely being illustrated scripturally (although illustration is one function of Scripture in Romans). Rather, logic and interpretation here interpenetrate to a remarkable degree and give Romans 9–11 a unique character within the Pauline corpus.[41] The questions therefore emerge: What is Paul doing here that makes the chapters distinctive? and Why does he do it? An-

---

39. Psalm 68:23, 24 in the Septuagint and 69:23, 24 in the Masoretic Text.

40. For the present purpose the scriptural allusions in the closing hymn in chap. 11, vv. 33–36, are excluded from consideration. The principles of interpretation at work there are nonetheless consistent with those elucidated by the present treatment.

41. Badenas, *Christ*, 90–92.

swers are forthcoming, when the purpose of Paul's argument is appreciated.

We would quickly decide that we understood what Paul is doing within this text and why he is doing it, were we able to accept the suggestion — developed in much recent scholarship — that Paul is here providing his readers with a Midrash.[42] It has become conventional to observe that the noun "Midrash" is derived from the verbal form *darash* (to "seek" or to "search" in Hebrew) and therefore to infer that "Midrash" refers to any "searching out" of meaning on the basis of Scripture within Judaism. It is fairly obvious that if one is willing to work with such a free-wheeling definition, Romans 9–11 is indeed "Midrash." But such a description obscures more than it discloses.

When the rabbis produced the documents known collectively as Midrashim, the formal aim was — on the whole — to produce commentaries on Scripture. But the "commentary" was not, as in modern usage, an attempt strictly (and historically) to explain the meaning of a given document. Rather, the sense that the rabbis explored in their Midrashim was the meaning of Scripture within their practice and liturgy and teaching, which were understood as of a piece with the Torah revealed to Moses on Sinai. That is, Midrash represents a synthesis of written text and rabbinic sensibility, in which both are accorded the status of revelation.

Jacob Neusner has written the most compelling, systematic account of the development and character of the Midrashim.[43]

---

42. See W. R. Stegner, "Romans 9:6–29 — A Midrash," *Journal for the Study of the New Testament* 122 (1984): 37–52. Stegner's work is essentially based upon that of E. Earle Ellis, *Paul's Use of the Old Testament* (Edinburgh: Oliver and Boyd, 1957), and idem, *Prophecy and Hermeneutic in Early Christianity* (Tübingen: Mohr, 1978). If recent discussion must qualify the description of Romans 9–11 as Midrash, there is nonetheless no doubt but that Ellis and Stegner contribute signally to our understanding of Paul's manner of thinking scripturally. Indirectly, the Midrashim shed light on the sort of activity Paul was engaged in; it is only the direct equation of Pauline interpretation with the genre of Midrash that needs to be set aside.

43. Jacob Neusner, *Midrash in Context: Exegesis in Formative Judaism,* The Foundations of Judaism 1 (Philadelphia: Fortress, 1983).

Among other things, he shows that a given Midrash may be composed of four distinct orders of interpretation:[44]

1. close exegesis, or discussion by each word or phrase of Scripture;

2. amplification of the meaning of a passage;

3. illustration of a particular theme by various passages; and

4. anthological collection around a general topic.

The result of the compilations of varying readings, involving different categories of interpretation, was the eleven distinct Midrashim (on various books of the Bible) that emerged by the end of the sixth century.[45]

When one sets out the Midrashim systematically and provides precise examples (as Neusner does), the distance from Paul's activity in Romans is striking. His focus is no single biblical book, so that the general form of Midrash is not at issue. The categories of exegesis and amplification, which Neusner shows were most prominent in the earliest Midrashim (of the second century C.E.), simply do not obtain in the case of Paul. It *might* be said — at a stretch — that the third and fourth categories do characterize Pauline interpretation. But the stretch is considerable because Paul does not merely illustrate by means of Scripture (although illustration is among his techniques); he argues through it and with it toward a conclusion that Scripture itself does not draw but — at best — is generally consistent with. And, of course, his overarching theme, of Jesus Christ's completion of the Torah, the Prophets, and the Writings, could never be described as rabbinic. For all those reasons, to style Paul's interpretation as "Midrash" is misleading.

Having called attention to the inadequacy of any direct identification of Paul's method with the rabbis', a certain analogy remains. Both proceed synthetically, and the synthesis moves in two directions at once. First, both take Scripture, as a whole,

44. Ibid., 82, 83. It should be noted that these are the modalities of interpretation that Neusner identifies in the Talmud and that he shows were then applied to the Bible in the Midrashim.
45. Ibid., 103.

as making a harmonious, common claim upon the mind.[46] Indeed, it should be pointed out that Paul specifies Torah first, and then the Prophets (by name) and the Writings, more punctiliously than the rabbis do. It appears that Paul wishes to make the point of Scripture's unity and also that he is making an inherently convoluted argument easier to follow than it would be if he were addressing genuine experts. Second, both Paul and the rabbis also synthesize Scripture with their own sensibilities, their grasp of what Scripture as a whole means.

The last point is perhaps best illustrated by how the rabbis of Leviticus Rabbah took the reference to Isaac in Gen. 21:12, which Paul in Rom. 9:7–8 interpreted to mean that the "children of promise" were the true "children of God." Instead, in Leviticus Rabbah, Abraham's seed is defined, without justification, as those who believe in the world to come.[47] What was for Paul obviously christological was for the rabbis (of a much later period) self-evidently a halakhah of eschatological belief. Just

---

46. For this reason, the procedures for associating disparate passages are important for both Paul and the rabbis. The famous rabbinic rules of interpretation might be regarded as an attempt to specify how the harmony of scripture may be defined; see A. Finkel, *The Pharisees and the Teacher of Nazareth,* Arbeiten zur Geschichte des Späjudentums und seiner Umwelt (Leiden: Brill, 1964), 123–28; Bruce Chilton and C. A. Evans, "Jesus and Israel's Scriptures," *Studying the Historical Jesus: Evaluations of the State of Current Research,* ed. Bruce Chilton and C. A. Evans, New Testament Tools and Studies 19 (Leiden: Brill, 1994), 281–335.

47. The following rendering is that of H. Freedman (*Genesis,* Midrash Rabbah, ed. H. Freedman and M. Simon [New York: Soncino, 1983]) at Gen. Rab. 53:12:

> AND GOD SAID UNTO ABRAHAM: LET IT NOT BE GRIEVOUS IN THY SIGHT . . . FOR IN ISAAC SHALL SEED BE CALLED TO THEE (21:12). R. Judah b. Shilum said: Not "Isaac," but IN ISAAC is written here. R. 'Azariah said in the name of Bar Ḥutah: The *beth* (IN) denotes two, i.e., [thy seed shall be called] in him who recognizes the existence of two worlds. R. Judah b. R. Shalum said: It is written, REMEMBER HIS MARVELOUS WORKS THAT HE HATH DONE, HIS SIGNS, AND THE JUDGMENTS OF HIS MOUTH (Ps. 105:5): [God says:] I have given a sign [whereby the true descendants of Abraham can be known], viz. he who expressly believes in the two worlds shall be called "thy seed," while he who rejects belief in two worlds shall not be called "thy seed."

In order to appreciate the interpretation, which also appears in the Talmud (Nedarim 31a), it is necessary to realize that ב (*beth*) in Hebrew may mean both "in" and "two."

when rabbinic and Pauline interpretation seem analogous, they prove they are antipodal.

Paul has also been compared to the sectarians of Qumran and to Philo, in respect of his interpretation of Scripture. But the famous *Pesherim* of Qumran are designed to relate Scripture exactly to the history of the community, and Philo is concerned to comment systematically on Scripture, so as to elucidate its allegedly philosophical truth.[48] Both the *Pesherim* and the Philonic corpus represent different activities and settings from Paul's: his scriptural interpretation strictly serves the protreptic function of Romans. He shows no sustained interest in historicizing Scripture (as in the *Pesherim*) or in philosophizing with it (as in Philo). Paul is driven by other motives, which is why Romans 9–11 is neither Midrash, *Pesher,* nor philosophical commentary.

Paul is arguing with all the Christians of Rome, both Jews and Gentiles, in an attempt to promote unity. It is true that Paul had no direct, personal acquaintance with the community at Rome; to that extent, there is an abstract quality about the letter to the Romans that sets it apart from other Pauline letters. Writing at a distance from a church known only at second hand, Paul approximates, more nearly than he ever does, to the presentation of his theology in a systematic fashion.[49]

Nonetheless, the central, social issue in the church at Rome was known to Paul: there had been disturbances involving Jews in the city, and probably Christians as well, that resulted in their being expelled in 49 C.E. under the Emperor Claudius.[50]

---

48. See Bruce D. Chilton, "Commenting on the Old Testament (with Particular Reference to the Pesharim, Philo, and the Mekilta)," in *It Is Written: Scripture Citing Scripture: Essays in Honour of Barnabas Lindars, S.S.F.,* ed. D. A. Carson and H. G. M. Williamson (Cambridge: Cambridge University Press, 1988), 122–40.

49. See E. P. Sanders, *Paul, the Law, and the Jewish People* (Philadelphia: Fortress, 1985), 31, 46, 59 n. 75, 97.

50. See Wolfgang Wiefel, "The Jewish Community in Ancient Rome and the Origins of Roman Christianity," in *The Romans Debate,* 100–119. Wiefel attempts to harmonize the accounts of the New Testament, Suetonius, and Dio Cassius, and in so doing may be reasoning beyond the limits of certainty imposed by the evidence. He argues that Claudius first expelled Jews from Rome (so Suetonius and Orosius) and — after many returned — attempted to prohibit their meeting in public (so Dio Cassius). F. F. Bruce imagines precisely the opposite scenario: meetings were first banned, and expulsion followed (*New Testament History* [London: Pickering and Inglis, 1982], 279–

The gradual reintegration of Jewish followers of Jesus into a single church with Gentiles, which is Paul's goal, could be accomplished only by means of conveying a coherent vision in which both Jews and Gentiles had a place.

The letter to the Romans offers just such a vision, which is summed up under the slogan that appears here, and only here, within the Pauline corpus: salvation is for the Jew first and then for the Greek (1:16; 2:9, 10; cf. 3:9, 29; 9:24; 10:12). Salvation is the possession of neither, but it is offered and granted to both as children of promise, provided it is accepted by means of a willingness to be forgiven.

His letter to the Galatians presents Paul in such heated controversy with Jews who were also Christians, and with those who demanded that the conditions of Judaism be fulfilled by all followers of Christ (whether Jew or Gentile), that one might have expected Paul to have used the occasion of his letter to the Romans finally to argue that the gospel of Christ could rightly be severed from its Judaic roots. Yet having written to the Galatians ca. 53 C.E., Paul went on in his Corinthian correspondence (ca. 55–56 C.E.) to appropriate scriptural stories of Israel's salvation directly for the Church (see, e.g., 1 Cor. 10:1–4) and even to put believing Christians in the role of teachers comparable to — if not greater than! — Moses (see 2 Cor. 3:7–18).[51]

Here, in Rome (ca. 57 C.E.),[52] was a case in which Judaism had been weakened to the point that Gentiles in the Church were tempted to imagine that the divine right of Israel had

---

83). But the fact of a disturbance involving Jews is well established; that it had an immediate impact upon Christianity is a sound inference (see Acts 18:2; Cassius Dio, *Roman History* 60.66; Suetonius, *Claudius* 25.4; Orosius, *Seven Books of History against the Pagans* 7.6). In any case, Wiefel is clearly correct in viewing Romans as an appeal for unity to a mixed church, in which Gentiles were in the majority. For further discussion, see E. Mary Smallwood, *The Jews under Roman Rule: From Pompey to Diocletian*, Studies in Judaism in Late Antiquity 20 (Leiden: Brill, 1976), 210–16 and Francis Watson, *Paul, Judaism and the Gentiles: A Sociological Approach*, Society for New Testament Studies Monograph Series 56 (Cambridge: Cambridge University Press, 1986), 91–94 (for positions in support of Bruce's).

51. Paul's position in Romans may be regarded as adumbrated in 1 Cor. 1:21–25; 9:20–23; 10:32, 33; 12:13; Gal. 3:28.

52. The dates here offered, which are well within the range of the scholarly consensus that has emerged, are those of Bruce D. Chilton, *Beginning New Testament Study* (Grand Rapids: Eerdmans, 1987).

been usurped definitively by the non-Jewish Church (cf. Rom. 11:13–24). Paul's response is unequivocal: the rejection of many in Israel does not give latecomers any special privilege. Indeed, the implication of the theology of the remnant is that the essential promise to Israel is confirmed, although the rebellion of some in Israel demonstrates that no one, Jewish or not, can presume upon God's gracious election. When Paul insists throughout Romans that salvation is to Jews first, and then to Greeks, the implication is that the same dynamics of redemption, initially worked out in the case of Israel, are now available to all humanity by means of Jesus Christ.

Romans 9–11 embodies that leitmotif in the letter generally. The salvation effected in Christ is uniquely comprehended by means of Scripture, where "Scripture" refers to the canon of Israel. When Paul turns to his gentile readers alone in 11:13–24, he momentarily drops any reference to Scripture and argues from an agricultural image.[53] His message is clear: however weak the Jewish component may appear, the Jews are root and you are branch. And it is all Israel, root and branch, that God is determined to save. Paul's purpose, once identified, explains both the nature and the form of his argument. The body of Christ is indeed the single definition of the Church, but the presence within it of some in Israel who believe is crucial even to Paul.

Hebrews

The particular contribution of Hebrews to the Christian interpretation of Scripture has already been characterized in volume 1 (pp. 165–67), with particular reference to chapter 9. Where the obvious question in what went before Hebrews (Paul included) was *the nature of Israel,* the natural question that emerges from Hebrews is *the nature(s) of Christ.* We can gauge

---

53. A. G. Baxter and J. A. Ziesler, "Paul and Arboriculture: Rom. 11:17–24," *Journal for the Study of the New Testament* 124 (1985): 25–32. Their argument is especially telling in that the purpose of the grafting — which was not considered outlandish in antiquity — was to reinvigorate the tree in which the scion was implanted. The authors (pp. 27–29) cite a contemporary of Paul's, Columella, *De re rusticus* 5.11.1–15, and *De arboribus* 26–27.

the magnitude of that change immediately by placing the "Israel" of Hebrews in the context of the often fraught, generative concern to define Israel within the movement of Jesus from its earliest phase.

Jesus had insisted upon a policy of treating all of Israel *as Israel*, pure enough by means of its customary practice to accept and enter the kingdom of God. For Peter, that made Jesus a new Moses: just as there is an implicit analogy between the followers of Jesus and the Israel that followed Moses out of Egypt, the prophetic covenant of Moses and the divine sonship of Jesus stand side by side, linked by their common source in the spirit of God. James's point of departure was David, rather than Moses. Here, the belief of Gentiles achieves, not the redefinition of Israel, but the *restoration* of the house of David, which is committed to preserve Israel in its purity. But Paul began with Abraham, who in Paul's theology embodied a principle of believing that was best fulfilled by means of faith in and through Jesus Christ. The Synoptic Gospels, in their variety, posit an *analogy* between Jesus and the figures of the Hebrew Bible. Christ becomes the standard by which Israel's Scripture is experienced, but not superseded; a separation between Jews and non-Jews remains. John's nuance is sophisticated but plain: Jesus is the true Israel, attested by the angels of God (see John 1:51), by whom all who believe might become children of God (see John 1:12–13).

All such options are brushed aside in Hebrews. The author understands Israel, literally, as a thing of the past, the husk of the first, now antiquated covenant. He says the word "Israel" just three times. Twice in chapter 8 he refers to Israel, but simply as part of his quotation of Jer. 31:31–34, where to his mind a completely new covenant is promised (Heb. 8:8, 10). The point of that citation, as elaborated by the author, is that the new covenant makes the former covenant obsolete (8:13). Accordingly, when the author speaks of Israel in his own voice, it is simply to refer to "the sons of Israel" in the past, at the time of the exodus from Egypt (11:22).[54] Melchizedek is a positive, theological

---

54. The reference is to Joseph's command for the disposal of his own bones, a fitting context for the attitude toward "Israel" in Hebrews!

category. Israel is no longer and remains only as a cautionary
tale from history.

The ability of the author of Hebrews to relegate Israel to
history is related to the insistence, from the outset of the
epistle, that the son's authority is greater than that of the Scripture. Once, God spoke in many and various ways through the
prophets; now, at the end of days, he speaks to us by a son
(Heb. 1:1, 2). The comparative judgment is reinforced when the
author observes that, if the word delivered by angels (that is,
the Torah)[55] carried with it retribution for transgression, how
much more should we attend to what we have heard concerning the son (Heb. 2:1–4). The implication of both statements is
clear: Scripture is only authoritative to the extent that it attests
the salvation mediated by the son (1:14; 2:3–4). The typology
that is framed later in the epistle between Jesus and the Temple
derives directly from the conviction of the prior authority of the
son of God in relation to Scripture.[56]

The dual revaluation, of Israel and Israel's Scripture, is what
permits Hebrews to trace its theology of Christ's replacement
of every major institution, every principal term of reference,
within the Judaisms of its time. Before Hebrews, there were
Christian Judaisms, in which Christ was in various ways conceived of as the key to the promises to Israel. The theology of
Hebrews proceeds from those earlier theologies, and it remains
a Christian Judaism, in the sense that all of its vocabulary of salvation is drawn from the same Scriptures that were axiomatic
within the earlier circles.

But the Christian Judaism of Hebrews is also and self-
consciously the expression of an autonomous Christianity, because all that is Judaic is held to have been provisional until the
coming of the son, after which point it is no longer meaningful. There is a single center within the theology of Hebrews.
It is not Christ with Moses, Christ with Temple, Christ with

---

55. The angelic mediation of the Torah was a common belief in the period;
see Gal. 3:19; Acts 7:53; Josephus, *Antiquities* 15 §136. See William L. Lane,
Hebrews 1–8 (Dallas: Word, 1991), 37–38.

56. See Barnabas Lindars, *The Theology of the Letter to the Hebrews* (Cambridge: Cambridge University Press, 1991), 38. Lindars also presents a careful
characterization of *how* the approach to Scripture in Hebrews might (and
might not) be called typological (pp. 53–55).

David, Christ with Abraham, Christ with Scripture, Christ with Israel. In the end, the center is not really even Christ with Melchizedek, because Melchizedek disappears in the glory of his heavenly archetype. Christ is the beginning, middle, and end of theology in Hebrews, just as he is the same yesterday, today, and forever (Heb. 13:8). Everything else is provisional — and expendable — within the consuming fire that is God (12:29).

Where even Paul allowed for an enduring place for Israel, an inclusion necessary for the promise to Abraham to be validated, the author of Hebrews conceives of the entire sacrificial system of Israel as a "shadow" of the substance to come (10:1). With the arrival of the substance, there is no need for shadow: "He abolishes the first in order to establish the second. And by that will we have been sanctified through the offering of the body of Jesus Christ once for all" (10:9b–10).

The closing of Hebrews invokes the name of Timothy (13:23) in a manner intended to imply Pauline authorship, but the epistle is more naturally associated with the sort of Alexandrine Christianity that produced Apollos, although it is to be dated later than Apollos.[57] But it is a logical extension of what the Pauline analysis pointed toward but never quite achieved.

The Revelation of John

Revelation was written at the close of the period during which the New Testament as a whole was composed. John of Patmos particularly developed themes that are sounded in the Gospel according to John, although his theological vocabulary is by no means limited to what he learned from that source. The identity of the writer is unknown, except that he wrote around the year 100 C.E. for churches in the vicinity of Ephesus (where John's Gospel was also composed).

The key to an understanding of Revelation is that it is what it says it is, an apocalypse (from the term *apokalupsis* in Greek), a disclosure of the heavenly court. In aid of the deliberately visionary medium of the work, the tone of intellectual argument

---

57. For further discussion, see Bruce D. Chilton and Jacob Neusner, *Judaism in the New Testament* (London: Routledge, 1995), 186–88.

(as, for example, in the letters of Paul) is avoided. Everything unfolds as a matter of what is seen and heard, rather than as a result of speculation. The very language of the document conveys its purpose; its Semitized Greek appears to be an artifice, a flaunting of the grammar even an elementary student would be aware of.

The lamb of God, an image used in the Fourth Gospel, is especially developed in the Revelation of John. When John the Baptist identifies Jesus as "the lamb of God which takes away the sin of the world" (John 1:29; cf. v. 36), an association with Passover is evident. It has been objected that the image of the lamb in itself is not necessarily paschal and that the removal of sin might more readily be associated with the daily offering (the *tamid*) than with the paschal lamb. When the image is taken in isolation, that observation is apposite. But paschal imagery permeates the Fourth Gospel with eucharistic meaning. The moment of Jesus' death in John corresponds to the time at which paschal lambs were normally slain: that Jesus was crucified during the afternoon of the day of preparation, just prior to Passover, is emphasized (19:14, 31). Moreover, John 19:36 cites a regulation concerning the paschal lamb, that no bone shall be broken (Exod. 12:46), in respect of Jesus' body on the cross. The sponge of vinegar raised on hyssop (specified only in John 19:29) may recollect the hyssop that was used to apply the paschal blood (Exod. 12:22).[58] The Johannine theology is specific: Jesus here is identified as the paschal lamb in 1:29, 36, just as he is identified as the true manna in 6:30–58.[59]

Jesus' discourse in John 6:30–58, in which he identifies himself as the true bread of life that must be eaten for eternal life, arouses opposition within his Jewish audience (see 6:41, 52) and even among the disciples (see 6:61). The eucharistic theology involved is obviously highly developed, as we have seen (pp. 141–143). Revelation takes up the paschal imagery of the Gospel within its own version of the Johannine portrayal of

---

58. See C. K. Barrett, *The Gospel according to St. John* (London: SPCK, 1960), 146–47; Raymond E. Brown, *The Gospel according to John*, The Anchor Bible (Garden City, N.Y.: Doubleday, 1966), 61–63.

59. See Ernst Haenchen *John 1*, trans. R. Funk, Hermeneia (Philadelphia: Fortress, 1984), 155, 156.

eucharist, as that which provokes controversy within Judaism. As noted above, the document itself is written in a Semitized Greek, with self-consciously bad grammar: some errors of case and tense, for example, are below a rudimentary level.[60] Such attempts at posing in the speech of a Judaic seer can scarcely convince when Jewish congregations are dismissed as instances of a "synagogue of Satan" (2:9; 3:9).

Separation from Judaism is also flagged in Revelation by a theological development: Jesus as the divine lamb is now explicitly an object of worship. The lamb of John 1:29, 36[61] has become a surreal "lamb standing as slain" (Rev. 5:6). The attribution of divine status to the lamb is obvious both in its placement — in the midst of the throne and the living creatures, among the elders — and in its possession of seven eyes "which are the spirits of God sent out into all the earth." The term used for "lamb" (*arnion*) connotes the helplessness of a lamb,[62] so that the fact of its slaughter is emphasized, yet the focus of Revelation is the power that proceeds from the lamb as a consequence of its slaughter. The lamb is worthy of heavenly and human worship (5:8, 13; 7:9–10) precisely as slain (5:12). That is the source of its authority to open the seals (5:1–5, 7; 6:1–2) and exercise judgment with God (6:15–16; see 14:9, 10; 17:12–14).

The essential focus of the Synoptic catechesis regarding eucharist, the solidarity of believers in the witness of a faithful martyr, is assumed in Revelation. Indeed, that solidarity is combined with the imagery of Jesus as a sacrifice for sin in the portrayal of Christian martyrs as those who have whitened

---

60. See R. H. Charles, *A Critical and Exegetical Commentary on the Revelation of St. John 1*, The International Critical Commentary (New York: Scribner's, 1920), cxvii–clix. The unique character of the Revelation's Greek style is well described on pp. cxliii, cxliv, but I cannot agree that the best explanation is that *"while he* (sc. the author) *writes in Greek, he thinks in Hebrew."* A more likely explanation is that "the author uses early Christian prophetic-apocalyptic traditions and understands the words of the book as prophetic *Geistrede* (speech of the Spirit)." See Elisabeth Schüssler Fiorenza, "The Quest for the Johannine School: The Book of Revelation and the Fourth Gospel," in *The Book of Revelation: Justice and Judgment* (Philadelphia: Fortress, 1989), 85–113, 106.

61. See Acts 8:32; 1 Pet. 1:19; Philip Edgcumbe Hughes, *The Book of the Revelation: A Commentary* (Grand Rapids: Eerdmans, 1990), 79, 80.

62. See Joachim Jeremias, "ἀμνός, ἀρήν, ἀρνίον," in *Theological Dictionary of the New Testament*, ed. G. Kittel, trans. G. W. Bromiley (Grand Rapids: Eerdmans, 1978), 338–41.

their robes in the blood of the lamb (7:14). They enjoy the presence of the lamb in their midst, now portrayed as shepherding them (7:17). It is telling that the image appears after reference to the sealing of the 144,000 of Israel (7:4–8) and to the worshiping throng "from every country, tribe, people, and tongue" (7:9–12). The union of Jewish and non-Jewish followers of Jesus within the heroic sacrifice, implicit within the Synoptics, is unmistakable within Revelation. The notion of whitening in blood is no paradox once it is understood that the underlying issue is the purification that Christ as sacrifice effects.[63]

Revelation 7 represents, in visionary form, the consensus of the New Testament regarding the global identity of the Church. The scope of the vision is marked by the number of the four angels, assigned to the four corners of the earth (7:1). Another angel arises to "seal" the servants of God, to mark them as slaves might be identified. Those marked first are 144,000 from Israel, 12,000 from each of the twelve tribes (7:2–8). Here, the image in the Gospels of twelve baskets gathered at the feeding of the five thousand has reached its apocalyptic climax (p. 139). Israel in the numerical structure of the biblical promise is guaranteed its place in the judgment that is to come.

The number seven, the number of the baskets associated with the feeding of the four thousand, is also central within Revelation, especially at this point in the book. The lamb is about to open the seventh and final seal in the presence of seven angels, to whom seven trumpets are given (8:1–2). As in the case of the feeding of the four thousand and the number of the deacons of the Hellenists in Jerusalem (p. 140), the number seven derives from the book of Zechariah, where "the seven eyes of the LORD" are said to "range through the whole earth" (Zech. 4:10). Seven is the number of the limitless reach of the divine kingdom. So here, in Revelation (as it happens, chap. 7), the perfected number of Israel is joined by "a great multitude which no one could number, from every nation — all tribes and peoples and tongues — standing before the throne and before the lamb, clothed in white robes with palm branches in their hands" (7:9).

---

63. See Charles, *Critical and Exegetical Commentary*, 213, 214.

Epilogue

In the Revelation of John, the language of vision accomplishes what the language of rational discourse could not. The definition of Israel had been a perennial problem because Jesus had not engaged in that conceptual issue in his emphasis on the emergence of the kingdom of God. He took Israel as he found it, in the interests of what he saw as the final, vindicating presence of God in Jerusalem, a Jerusalem open to all the nations.

The absence of Israel from Jesus' teaching left his most influential followers to address the conceptual question of Israel's proper role. For James, worship in Jerusalem was at the heart of the movement, and the restoration of the house of David was its divine purpose. Non-Jews could offer support but not leadership. The community of Q, for all the opposition it encountered within Israel, did not deviate from a focus on how that Israel would fare in the ultimate judgment.

From the point of view of Paul, Peter's practice represented and encouraged confusion (at best), but his position finally triumphed. Without in any way denying Israel's place as the continuing people of God, Peter insisted on the grounds of his experience that God had also bestowed his spirit on non-Jews in baptism. That contention was worked out in a consistent fashion by Barnabas, whose Levitical background in Cyprus resulted in an enhanced concern for the purity of Israel in the midst of the nations.

Paul's insistence (in Galatians) that faith in Jesus was the true definition of the sons of Abraham (see Gal. 3:7) would appear logically to replace Israel with those who believe in Jesus. That outcome seems to be pursued in Paul's development of the concept of "the body of Christ," and Hebrews represents the logic of replacement in its most developed form. But Paul himself, in Romans 9–11, curiously backs away from that logic when he concentrates on the question of Israel itself. In the end, he embraces the position of Peter that Israel is not in fact obliterated by the new effulgence of spirit that faith in Jesus represents.

The history of Christianity has seen countless examples of thinkers who have tried to be more Pauline than Paul (even more Pauline than the "Paul" of Hebrews!). The most famous of them is Marcion, the second-century teacher who attempted to produce a canon of Scripture laundered of Judaic content and influence.[64] But those efforts run against the grain of the New Testament, which represents only experiments with the hypothesis that Israel is irrelevant, experiments whose results largely negate the hypothesis. In the thought of Jesus, James, the community of Q, Peter, Barnabas, Paul himself, and the author of Hebrews, Israel remains a focus, however far beyond Israel the promise to Abraham may extend.

Indeed, without the promise of Israel, understood as Jesus' anticipation of the kingdom of God, there is no Church. To be a member of a congregation, a church, is to be called out from one's ordinary preoccupations, to join those who discern the hand of the single God, the God of Israel, actively engaged in one's world. By definition, to belong to one such congregation is to belong to them all, to the Church at large,[65] because precisely one God is worshiped in each. Paul's brilliant development of the concept of the body of Christ articulates, simply and canonically, how we who believe in Jesus, in our churches as well as in the Church as a whole, belong to one another even as we belong to our Lord.

The Lord we belong to is defined by Israel, although he himself did not draw the boundaries of Israel. His Israel was not over and against another group, nor a matter of a single social constitution, but the place of purity where God's kingdom could be encountered, celebrated, anticipated. That Israel is always at the heart of the Church; and the Church realizes its identity as it engages in dialogue with all who honor biblical Israel.

---

64. See Chilton, *Beginning New Testament Study*, 14–15.
65. The Greek term *katholike* (catholic) originally designated the Church in just this sense, not denominationally.

Index of Biblical and Talmudic References

General Index